CONTROVERSIAL DREAMS WISHES HOPES LYRICS

Part 1

by
Garry William Gosney

Controversial Dreams Wishes Hopes Lyrics Part 1

garrygosney@yahoo.com

© 2000 - Current date Garry William Gosney

© Perth Desperado

A World of Poetry

Garry Gosney

FROM... UNORTHODOX AUSTRALIAN POET

Garry Gosney

Copyright *1998 / to current DATE

ISBN – Ebook: 978-1-923493-03-2

ISBN - Paper Back: 978-1-923493-04-9

ISBN - Hard Cover: 978-1-923493-05-6

ABN: 62289687418.

Garry Gosney

To Someone ever so Special

You are special for you are my friend

You're the beauty in my life

For without you my friend I am nothing

God bless you my friend

May our friendship continue to prosper

For the true beauty is having you for my friend

Ti Amo forever more

Controversial Dreams Wishes Hopes Lyrics Part 1

My Dedication

To my family,

Even though we are worlds and thousands of miles apart You will always be in my heart and my prayers and you have my love.

To all my friends who told me to publish these Without their encouragement none of this would have been possible.

Special Thanks to,

Special Thanks To Independent Country Music Artists Rory Ruff All my internet friends for their support over the years And for their push and perseverance with me when I needed it They are special Without them it would have been impossible as they are some of my biggest inspiration But the one that deserves the credit is GOD Without his help none of this would ever be possible And I thank the publishers for taking me on I hope you all like and that the words come out all right Please feel free to email me anytime with your comments.

Garry Gosney

Table of Contents

My Dedication iv

I See a Rainbow 1

Finding the Time 2

Northern Star of Beauty 4

Wedding Card 5

Your Worth 7

The Greatest Gift 8

A Rose for You 9

Ti Amo My Special One 10

Somewhere Along the Way 11

Every Corner I Turn 12

Darling I Know 13

The Hardest Answers 14

So Young Yet So Pretty 16

This Old Fool 17

Controversial Dreams Wishes Hopes Lyrics Part 1

Just What Will It Take 18

Weakness or Strength 19

Just What Power 20

The Long Road of Life 21

I'm a Fool in Love 23

Voice of an Angel 24

To See You Smile One More Time 25

Words I Can Not Find 26

I Call It Justified 28

The Warmth and Beauty of My Lady 31

Diary of a Lonely Heart 32

And My Heart Skips a Beat 34

The Trucker's Run 36

My Little Trucker's Prayer 38

Special Time a Special Memory 40

The Christmas Season 42

Garry Gosney

It's Christmas Time 44

Love For My Lady 45

My Love For You My LADY 46

The Spirits Watch 48

Heavens Smiling Down Me 49

The True Beauty 51

So Many Things 53

Hours That Seem to Never End 54

The Ocean Has My Heart 55

Nothing Can Mend 56

The Ones in Power 59

A Season to Remember 61

The Price Is the Same 63

53 State Little America 65

Wanted One Beautiful Imperfection 68

Ordinary Man Dreams 70

Controversial Dreams Wishes Hopes Lyrics Part 1

Ti Amo My Friend 71

Hearts Do Talk If You Believe 72

A Person's Word of Trust 74

Torn Between 77

The True Wild Flower of Life 80

My Driving Force 81

While I Have a Today 83

Voice That Has Painted a Picture 85

My Door Is Always Wide Open 86

The Voice of Beauty 87

An Angel in Disguise 88

My Perfect Night 89

Beautiful Music 91

Look at You Girl 92

Dancing to the Call 94

Two Strangers with One Heart 95

Garry Gosney

Aged Before Your Time 96

Good to Be Home 98

Tranquility of the Land 100

A Dream with a Meaning 101

Seem Like Heaven 103

But.. 104

A Dream No More 105

A Scarred Heart 106

Different Drums 107

Remember Where You Come From 108

Dream of a Thousand Tears 110

Remember I Love You Always 111

My World Changed 112

The Fourth of July 113

My First Fourth of July 2002 117

Number One in Me 120

Controversial Dreams Wishes Hopes Lyrics Part 1

I Dream of 121

A Gift With A F.L.A.W. 122

My Special Friends My Children 124

A Ghost, a Shadow Without Meaning 126

Sorrow but Happiness 128

Promise 129

Time Is Short 130

CHERISHED 131

God 132

Shooting Star 133

My Everything My All 134

ONE 135

My Mountain Home 136

OWN 137

Nightmare of Tears 138

The Saddest Song of All 139

Garry Gosney

My Heart No More 141

Every Time 142

Sparkle 144

The Ghost That Prayers 145

She Is 146

Existence 147

11 September 2002 A Year Ago Today 148

This Land My Home 150

Happy Birthday 151

Oh What a Lady 154

Just How Can I 158

Garry Gosney

I See a Rainbow

Listening to and watching the rain falling Listening to the rhythm of the rain

All I can think of you is thousands of miles away Many a time I'm glad of the rain and the rainbow

I see a rainbow and send you my wish and my love

For the tears of love I shed the rain covers up For you are always in my heart no matter what Why did you have be so plain, yet oh so beautiful

Why did you have to be so imperfect yet so beautiful I see a rainbow and send you my wish and my all

I close my eyes and just listen to the falling rain My heart cries for the heart it's longing for Wondering just what I did to ever to deserve you

For you are far more beautiful then I could ever say I see a rainbow and send you my wish and my heart

I prayed for a dream to come true and got a miracle I wished on a star and I found them in your eyes

I see a rose and I see the most beautiful flower of all

I see you so imperfect in everyway, but that makes you Makes you so oh so beautiful to me, "my perfect rose" I see a rainbow and send you my love and my heart

I see a rainbow and wish that someday you will be mine Someday you will except the little I have to give

I see a rainbow and wish you can feel my love tonight I see a rainbow and send you my wish and my heart

I see a rainbow and ask it to protect my perfect rose "You"

Controversial Dreams Wishes Hopes Lyrics

Finding the Time

Love is not what you say or how you say it Love is not what you rite or how you rite it

Love is not a tap you turn on and of when you like Love is about a lot of little things many that go un-noticed

Little things that over time we all take for granted

Just reminiscing over the little things that made us fall in love

But as always over time the little thing we did for love We did for love turn into the things we take for granted

We forget to live for love for love for we take it for granted We live for the sake of living and knowing that we are needed But we hang on to our security blanket for fear of the unknown

I wonder how many stay for the sake of their security blanket

I wonder just how many stay just for the sake of knowing their needed I wonder just how many know what made them fall in love in the first place What made us loose the spark, that fire in our hearts, just were did it go Just how and why did we fall out of love and do we want it back as it was

We can go on forever on the just wonderings but what are we holding on too Holding on to a letter of a lover to get you through the day and nights Holding on to a memory of a lover to get you through the day and nights Holding on to a lot of maybes or might have been or could have been Were did we go wrong just what was the turning point of no return

It's not about words but about finding the time to show you care about someone

A rose or a flower every now and then just to let her know how you care for her

Or a note just to say 3 little words "I Love You"

It don't take or cost much to show you care for someone or love them

Garry Gosney

It's finding the time to do the little things to show you care

It's the time that you make for each other that is most important the little things

The little things that say "I Love You"

Controversial Dreams Wishes Hopes Lyrics

Northern Star of Beauty

Sitting and listening to the sounds of the nightlife Listening to sounds of the night owls and the night birds calling

Watching to stars dance their dance to the southern skies Seeing them dance the most perfect dance of all

Seeing them dance amongst the clouds so soft and swift Seeing them sparkle against the dark of night

Ever so soft, ever so bright but dancing a slow waltz

I can not dance but I see the stars dancing and I think of you I watch you dance around the room oh so beautiful to see

I shed a tear for I hope your dancing with me in you're heart I can not dance but my heart is dancing every step with you I see the stars dancing and all I see is you

I hear your voice and my heart cries out to hold you

I see you dance and my heart cries out to dance the love waltz with you The sounds of nightlife just makes my heart yearn to make you mine Can a northern star ever fall in love with a southern cloud

If I could I wrap you up and never let you go, but how can I make you stay How can I make you stay when all I want to do is see you dance a slow waltz

Maybe someday you will teach me the dance of love the slow waltz The slow waltz my heart does every night when I see the stars dance their dance

The slow dance of love, but all I can think of is how to make you stay How can I make someone worth so much stay with someone that has nothing but love

The northern star of beauty and the southern cloud dancing the slow waltz of love

Garry Gosney

Wedding Card

To the LOVE Birds

—and—

Today my heart and I am sad

For today two of my best friends are celebrating

—and—this is your day of days night of nights Their celebrating marriage of two hearts as one

Today I am sad my Lady and I could not be there on your day We are so proud and happy that they found each other

So happy they are as one and may God look after you both May God look after you both as one in heart and body

For they are special friends to us now and forever

We can not be there in person but our hearts are watching May your day this wedding day of two people as one And two hearts as one be blessed with all the piece

The piece and happiness and harmony a marriage should be May each day be a wedding day and may each night be ???? The night well ???? Their yours we do not want to know about But what you both do please do it together as one

And may God be kind to you both and the angels watch over you May your health and everything you hold dear be blessed as well But no matter what ever you do or what happens never forget Your friends are always close and a call away

Dial a phone number or net call what ever you choose we are around

May your life be as bright as fireworks on the 4th of July May the fireworks of the heart never stop

Hope you both have many happy days and nights to come May the

Controversial Dreams Wishes Hopes Lyrics

hours be kind

Love to you both from

Garry Gosney

Your Worth

*"Life is only a heart beat away" "Love is only a heart beat away"
"Beauty is only a heart beat away"*

"The beauty of the heart is seeing from within" "The beauty of the heart is knowing you"

"Just remember if I am not worth that much"

"Your worth 10% of what I am not that much "God Bless You"

"What are you worth"

Controversial Dreams Wishes Hopes Lyrics

The Greatest Gift

Many days and nights I long to be at your side Many days and nights I long to hold you in my arms Walking hand in hand nowhere special just walking Just being with you gives my life a meaning a purpose

Just seeing you smile, hearing your voice Just feeling your touch, looking into your eyes

All I can see is a gift and a true miracle

How can one improve on the gift of love God gave you How can one improve on the gift of beauty that I love Mother Nature gave you her all the gift of outer beauty But most of all she gave you the precious gift of all

The most precious gift of all is your beauty from with in Between Mother Nature and God they gave you the greatest gift The gift of all gifts to be a mother, a lover, a friend

But to me the greatest gift of all is in loving you for you

TI AMO

Garry Gosney

A Rose for You

1 red rose for the love I have for you 1 red rose for the beauty in loving you

1 red rose for each year you share my heart

1 red rose for being you just as only you can be 1 red rose for the tears you shed because of me

1 red rose for each of you're special days we share

1 white rose to show you the purity of my love

1 white rose for each year of happiness you give me 1 white rose for all the tears and hurt I've done

1 white rose for being apart of my heart

1 white rose for each of you're special days we share

1 yellow rose for your hand in mine

1 pink rose for the beauty of your friendship 1 blue rose for the heartache you bring me

6 red and white rose for you are the world to me

1 dozen red roses for the love I have for you 1 dozen white roses for my love for you is pure

1 dozen kiss for you deserve much more than I can give

Controversial Dreams Wishes Hopes Lyrics

Ti Amo My Special One

I love you for ever I will be yours. Beside you always I will stand

Just how many times can one say it

How many times must I say it for you to believe Believe that you are the only one I ever need

The only one I long to hold for you are part of me

So many times I have tried to say what you mean to me So many ways I have tried, but you never seam to hear I've never wanted to hurt you only wanted to love you Thousands of miles away but my heart is with you

Many a tear I shed for I just don't know what to do A thousand tears I shed for I can't make you see

See that I love you and that you mean the world to me What can I do to show you that you have my heart my all

But I guess I don't have what it takes

But you can bank on this I will never stop loving you

I have nothing to offer you, but with you I have everything You are everything my heart desires, everything I hoped for You are a dream come true; I will never stop loving you

Ti Amo…Ti Amo…Forever and a day Ti Amo my special one…Ti Amo

Garry Gosney

Somewhere Along the Way

You noticed me once and we loved

We lived and loved a lot in the time we shared

I lived and saw you grow and blossom into something Something oh so beautiful that only a rose could Could and would enhance your beauty, plain yet oh so Oh so beautiful and special to me in every way

We lived and loved a lifetime in such a short time We seen each other laugh and cry but we learnt a lot We seen each other though the good times and the bad

But somewhere along the way you drifted but I stayed But I will always stay on the side for you are my life You are all I ever need for you are a special part of me A special part of me that time will never erase

For time is the best part of the heart

For the heart has no time and the heart knows no boundaries

We lived and loved a lifetime in such a short time We seen each other laugh and cry but we learnt a lot We seen each other though the good times and the bad But somewhere along the way you drifted and I stayed

Controversial Dreams Wishes Hopes Lyrics

Every Corner I Turn

I go out but every corner I turn every place I go I see your face and hear your voice

Then I shed a tear for I know it's not you I shed a thousand more on the inside

Not even sunglasses can cover up the tears I cry My eyes can see the pain my heart is in over you

Not a day or night goes by that they do not cry a tear Cry a tear for you for they know what you mean to me

I hear my name and all I hear is your voice so soft I see you in every place I go and everyone I meet I see them talking but I only hear you

I see them but I only see you, then my heart cries out

I see a rose and I can only think of your beauty

I see a carnation and I can only think of your soft touch But when you put them both together the perfume is oh so Oh so special oh so magnificent like the stars in your eyes

Then I shed a thousand more for I know you are not there My heart cries a thousand more for it does not know what to do I cry for my love for you is real but it dose not good

Does no good for you don't care you just walk on by to another And my heart cries a thousand more, but what for, cause I love you

Garry Gosney

Darling I Know

Darling I know that I am not the one you wont Some say I am a fool for loving you the way I do I close my eyes and I only see you

My eyes are wide-open put I only see you

I look in to the mirror and all I see is me a fool A fool in love with an image, a picture, a memory

I see you at your worse "first thing in the morning" I see you at night when your worn out and tired

I look into the mirror and I can not think of a reason Not one reason can I think of why you could ever love me

I look around me and I can see nothing but emptiness

I look around and I see your picture and my heart cries out to you

Darling all I can do is laugh for you are beautiful

Not a minute or an hour goes by that you are not beautiful to me When you work or play, laugh or cry or just covered in mud your You're special oh so special to me even knowing I'm not the one you want

Darling I'd give a penny for your thoughts, a shilling for your dreams Darling I'd give a pound for some say I am a fool for loving you But I hope that in time you will see that this fool is in love with you I close my eyes I see you, eyes wide open I see you

This heart of a fool knows the why I love you This heart of a fool knows you love another but not me But how does a fool stop loving you with their heart

Controversial Dreams Wishes Hopes Lyrics

The Hardest Answers

Some ask me what I am looking for and what I want In one way it is easy to say the answer

But in another way it's the hardest answer to give

...answers...

I go looking for something

I go wanting a heart to call mine

I go expecting nothing but wanting something

I go looking for something

A place to call my own and be me You have nothing I really need

For I have nothing I can really give you

I go wanting a heart to call my own

A imperfect heart it can be for mine is imperfect

I can only give you what I have my heart and my love I can only give you what I can

I go expecting nothing but wanting something I go asking you for your heart and love

I go giving you my heart and my love my all

I do not expect anything from you that I cannot give you

Nothing will change the love I have for you Nothing will change the way I see and feel inside for you Nothing will change my heart as it is, only you will change Only you will change your mind but my heart will go on

My heart will go on loving you as my heart always has and will I give you my heart for you're heart

I give you my love for your love

I give you nothing and want nothing

Garry Gosney

I give you what I can afford and my love, my heart I just hope I can get a little bit back someday

I can only ask for what I can give you in return

Ti Amo Forever

Controversial Dreams Wishes Hopes Lyrics

So Young Yet So Pretty

I look at you and I see a beauty like no other

I see your eyes and watch how you make them smile I see you move around in the distance

So young, plain and pretty in your own way

So young, yet so pretty and yet so trouble You try hard to laugh away the tears you shed You try hard to smile away the pain you have

So young, yet so strong and in away innocent too

I see you cry, but you always say your not and I laugh For every time you cry your nose gives you away

For every time you cry your eyes do not smile

You try so hard to cover up your tears but they add to you

But in their own way they add to your beauty

The way you look, the smiling eyes, the way you hold your head They all add to the beauty of knowing and loving you

They are a gift from God and Mother Nature

The cheeky way you smile and laugh makes you one of a kind

:) stick that tongue back in :) before you bite it off They all add to making you what you are simple and plain But most of all they make you beautiful in your own way

They add to the beauty of knowing you for they are part of you

Garry Gosney

This Old Fool

When the girl in your arms is the girl in your heart When you're holding your dream that you've been dreaming

Then you got everything, you're a rich as a king

I see you and all I want to do is to hold close Years a part we me maybe that is so true but I can't help

Help feeling and wondering what you see in me All I see is an old fool in love with you a puppy :) Why I will never know what you see in me

But I know you make feel good inside when ever I see you

Thousands of miles and oceans apart we maybe But when I see you I feel as close as I can be

I bring you to me in a dream and hold you oh so close

I hear your voice, see your smile and I don't want it to end I reach out to touch your hand in mine and I think of just Just how rich you've made me feel and oh so proud of you So proud to love you and to hold you in my arms

All I see is an old fool in love with you a puppy :) Why I will never know what you see in me

But I know you make feel good inside when ever I see you

Then I wake up only to know it's a dream

A thousand tears I cry for I cannot be were I want to be A thousand more for in my dream I never leave you

A thousand tears I cry for I cannot understand what you see What you see in this old fool that's in love with you

Controversial Dreams Wishes Hopes Lyrics

Just What Will It Take

What will it take to show you I care and love you What will it take to show you what you mean to me Just what will it take

I can promise you the moon I can promise you the world

I can promise you anything you would like But if I did that it would be a lie

There is only one promise I can make to you But will it be enough, just what will it take

Will it take a rose every now and then that I can give Will it take a walk holding hand in hand

Will it take wiping away the odd tear or two Will it take a cuddle and I love you

These are the things I know and can promise to give you But will it be enough to show you how much you mean to me

Just what will it take a promise I can not give you a lie The truth is I can only give what I can and no-more

"a rose, a kiss, a cuddle, just the simple things" But will it be enough to keep your love

Just what will it take

Garry Gosney

Weakness or Strength

They say it's ok to admit your weak

They say it's ok to admit it because we only human But the only problem is they never said it hurts so much

So to make mistakes mean we weak

We all make mistakes but some more then others Guess what I'm the more it seams to be my pass time

I wonder if admitting to making them makes us stronger

I wonder what others think of the weak or if it really matters Is it weak to want to be loved by someone

Is it weak to want to know that you need to belong

Is it a weakness or is the strength that is in knowing you're loved Just what is the strength of our weakness is it a sign from God A sign that we need help and a weakness in us to ask him to help Just what does it mean

"weakness in our strength "and" strength in our weakness" Just what strange powers and gifts dose it hold for us Will the ones we care about ever forgive our weakness

Will they ever understand our weakness and our strengths Maybe someday with gods help they might

But most importantly can we ever forgive and understand ourselves

Is it a weakness or strength to admit that you need to blong That you need to be loved by the ones you care about the most if you need somebody your week

that's what makes you strong that's what makes us week

Controversial Dreams Wishes Hopes Lyrics

Just What Power

Love just what power does it have Just how far will we go

How far will we look the other in the name of love Does it have the power to turn the strong to weak Does it have the power to turn the weak into strong Just what power does love have over us

Many a time we turn a blind eye to their weakness Many a time we only look for the strength in others Many a time we often over look the little things The funny and sad things that made us fall in love Just how far will we go

Just what power does love have over us

Is it wrong to love the simple little things in life To wipe away the odd tear or two when needed

To hold out a hand and give a hug when you feel like it To give a kiss, to give a smile, just how far will we go Just how far did God go

Just how far will we go

Just how far will we take the power of love Just how far can we go

Will we stay with in our limit or go beyond Will we be something we're not

Just to find piece of heart, piece of mind and love Love just what power does it have

Just what power lies within the heart

Garry Gosney

The Long Road of Life

The road is long and slow

The road is winding in and around You have three forks in the road The right, the middle, the left

The right is for the rich and famous

The middle is for the ones born with a silver spoon The left is for the ones that get trodden on by the way

They all start at the same the spot in life But just what road do we take

They all end at the same spot in life The long and hilly road of the poor

The long and winding road of the silver spooners Or the long straight road of the rich

Does it really matter what road we take so long So long as we lend a hand to a friend in need Give a smile and lend a heart when its called for The long straight road is full of rich fakes

They give not for it's good but for a tax dodge The winding road is full of people trying to be

Trying to be what there not but hope they can pass The hilly road of the poor is a funny road

It's the longest of all

Their road is long and winding with hills and straights They can stop and see the cites and no one cares

They can be nowhere but be everywhere

They are forever offering a hand or a heart whenever needed Yep to some it cost a lot but they give it freely

Why is it we are all born on the same long road of life Why is it we all die on the same long road of life

Controversial Dreams Wishes Hopes Lyrics

But most importantly is what road we take and why we do it

I have lived on all side of the fence and traveled all the roads But to me the most beautiful road is the road I took to see you The poor mans road is the best for the scenery is so full of natural Natural beauty a gift that God gave us to share with others along the way

To help others from were ever they come from to see the beauty of life

But most of all I thank God for showing me the road to you

Garry Gosney

I'm a Fool in Love

Just how many times have we dreamed Dreamed a dream of love and happiness Only to find that we are a only fools Fools to believe in love and what it brings

How many time have you loved someone Only to find they love someone else

Only to be used and played like a fool in love

Only to find your in love with someone not in love with you

How many times must your heart be broken Just how long will it take for you to learn Maybe never for if loving you makes me a fool Then that makes me the biggest fool of all

How any times have you waited home for a call How many time have you gone out only to be alone Only to find out that the one you want is not there How many times must our hearts get broken

If loving you is wrong then I don't want to be right If loving you makes me into a fool then I'm it

But this fool with a broken heart is in love with you Just remembering the good times with you makes me a fool

Just dreaming of loving and happiness with you makes me a fool Then I can only say I'm fool in love, in love with you

Controversial Dreams Wishes Hopes Lyrics

Voice of an Angel

I close my eyes and see you there

I reach out to you and hold your hand Only to find you're not there

I hear the phone ringing and I hope it's you

I hear your voice but it seams sad for some reason It's like you've been crying a tear or two

But hoping that I would never find it in your voice But it's that funny little tear in your voice

That tear that gives you away

Darlin' I wish I could be there with you but I can't But in away I am and you're with me

You're in my heart so don't shed a tear but listen Listen to our hearts talking and comforting each other Darlin' oceans and many miles apart we maybe

But not matter what we have each other our heart are one I hear your voice but it seams sad for some reason

Darlin' do cry but listen to your heart talking

That funny little tear in your voice That tear that gives you away

I close my eyes and I draw you near to me and hold you tight I look into your eyes and kiss away your tears

My funny little clown with tears in her voice A voice of an angel

Ti Amo my little clown, my darlin' angel

Garry Gosney

To See You Smile One More Time

Just to see you smile one more time What I would give just to see you smile

I gave you my heart but you knocked it back I gave you my love but you did not want it

I see you smile but I know it's for another What I would give to have you smile one more time The thing is I can give you nothing for I have nothing Nothing for everything I have tried you have blocked

What would it take to make you smile for me one more time I have nothing to give you that's true

I give you my love and you block it and throw it away

I give you my heart only to have you throw it away like trash

We all make mistakes and some more than others I make plenty Believe me I make enough for twenty or more, but that's me I shed a thousand tears just to see you smile for me one last time Just what would it take to see you smile one more time

I give you my heart but it's not what you want I give you my love but it's not what you want

I give you my all what little it may be but it's not enough I give you me only to find you throw it all away

I shed a thousand tears for I wish I could give you a miracle I shed a thousand more for I cannot give you what you want But you will always have the gift of knowing someone loves you

Controversial Dreams Wishes Hopes Lyrics

Words I Can Not Find

Many a time I long to hold you Many a time I reach out for you I feel my heart dancing with you

I close my eyes and can see you dancing I try to think of us as one in love

One love, one heart dancing the love waltz But sadly I can not for I can not dance

A candle light dinner for two

I look into your eyes but something is missing I look at the stars but I see you

I try to talk but the words just don't come out I try to make it a perfect night

I shed a thousand tears on the inside

For I can not find the right time or the right words I go out side in the rain to cry so no one will see

No one can see the tears I cry for the words I can not find I see a shooting star and make a wish

To me any night with you is a perfect night To me any day with you is a perfect day

But I can still not fine to perfect words to say what What you mean to my heart and just how much you mean to me

I thank God for giving me you

I thank Mother Nature for making you as beautiful as she is I ask them both to give me the words

But I just can't seam to see or find them, the words to say Say just how much you mean to me and my heart .

How do you find the perfect time to say "I Love You" When anytime with you is perfect

Garry Gosney

I go out side in the rain to cry so no one will see

No one can see the tears I cry for the words I can not find The right words to say "I Love You"

Ti Amo For Ever

Controversial Dreams Wishes Hopes Lyrics

I Call It Justified

21 days ago a friend I went to see my solicitor

I had to take in some paperwork she wanted signed And I rote on it settlement 1 December and I mean it

Cash in hand :) or we go to court and she can earn her money I trust her as far as I can kick her so I took a friend

We asked her to rite a letter up for the government She said my file was sent a week ago to get costed It should that 7 to 10 days to get back...that was ok

That makes 21 + 7 = 28 days so being good I gave them 14 days 28 - 14 = 14days ago I should of had the letter I asked for

I have emailed her 3 or 4 times asking for the letter I rang her 3 or 4 times and asked for it as well

This will be the 9th time all up I have asked for it

It's a great law firm when you have to ask 9 times for anything 9 times the cost of the firm is worth .

It's the only way they can make a profit As they can not do it any other way

You ask them once and once only you pay them once not 9 times They are only worth 1 tenth of what I am paying them

As that is all the work they have done .

They have not done one thing I have asked once .

I hate to think of how many more pensioners they have ripped off Or how many more they will get away with just so they can profit Suncorp insurance company no longer has any more of my business Nor will any of the associates if I find out who they are

And I told all my friends to stay clear of them As they treat you like crap...a number .

Garry Gosney

The doctors involved in this case are as useless as tits on a bull The physiologists in the case all they were interested in was more More psychological rape and see how much money they can get.

As for being professionals at what they do. I would not recommend them I could not recommend any of them as not one did any thing to fix it

If anything they have all made it 10 times worse .

*So should be paid ten times least for a service not one provided And the **POLITICIANS** let them get away with it*

The law society lets them get away with it The medical profession lets them get away with it

The law is over 200 yrs old dating back to the convict days When the queen sent her convicts here so she did not have to feed them But 200 years later the queen want them to spend 20mill to see her ever time Shows how far stupidity goes back hey . and how far the corruption dose

200 years and we have learnt nothing .

200 years and the law has not got it's head out off the sand The rich get richer and the poor get poorer

And the ones on a disability or a pension get used and abuse and walked on

And the law lets them get away with it its call justified Justified because they are educated . Justified because they are professionals

80 percent of the professionals would not know if the ass was on fire unless Unless someone told them…they all get paid 9 times more than they should

Because they think they are Gods gift to what / who ever of the crap heap maybe

But not of me . No one walks on me and gets away with it any more I'm an Aussie with an attitude.

I never forget. I never forgive. I only tolerate.

Controversial Dreams Wishes Hopes Lyrics

And I let you know.

Not one of you in my case can use the words reputable and professional Because I have never seen any of it showing

And cannot recommend you to a flea never alone a human being

And I call it justified...

Garry Gosney

The Warmth and Beauty of My Lady

Today I sat and watch for the first time beauty of my lady coming to life To see her for the first time was like watching a miracle of Mother Nature It was like watching a flower bud opening up into sunlight for the first time Its great to see her beauty come to life like the suns rays in the morning sky As the day gets older the more prettier she becomes and shines like the sun As the day get older her warmth shines through to make you feel needed As the day turns into night and the chill of the night air starts to come in Her warmth is there to comfort you in every way she make a home a home The warmth of her smile, the warmth of her tender touch

The warmth of a kiss, the warmth of her body just being there The warmth of her love, the warmth of being a friend when needed The list is endless, but the warmth of her beauty is so special and precious

Each day I thank God for giving her to me

Each day I thank God for showing me her true beauty the beauty with in Each day that her beauty grows and her warmth get stronger and stronger Each day and night I look for a fault but I can only see a miracle of nature Every time I see her all I ever see is beauty the beauty God gave to her Her smile and love and everything about her make you want to believe in God

Make you want to believe in miracle and that they exist and can come true She does not ask for much in return just that you love her for her self That you love her for the woman that she is

To me she is pure beauty and joy to be with every moment together Is a moment I cherish with all my heart and is a moment I share with God

Together we share her beauty and her love and her warmth

Controversial Dreams Wishes Hopes Lyrics

Diary of a Lonely Heart

Day one I just sit and wait waiting to see her come home...Sunday

Trying to talk to her every chance I get that precious Time together we call our own 5 mins or 10 mins or an

hour or 2 it is our time to be together with the one we love She is on holidays now so it is had I long for her

long for her company her sound but know it will not come I hope my lady is having a wonderful time doing what

ever my lady likes...with in reason...hee hee hee that's my lady

I sit and wait for that phone call to come...Monday day two arrived I get a call my angel spoke to me I rang her back I spoke to the angel of my dreams I hoped she would have a good and great holiday

after all a beautiful lady deserves a wonderful time I just wish I was there just for her so I could see her see her smile, see her laugh, and watch her play She is my dream

Day three arrived and still no call no angel no voice...Tuesday Tonight I rang her and spoke to the woman of my dreams

it was so beautiful to hear her sweet sweet voice

a voice of the angel I love so dear and close to my heart The beautiful woman is my lady to me that sweet smile that soft voice that gentle touch

Day four arrived and still no call no angel no voice...Wednesday

Tonight she rings that ever so beautiful sweet voice We talked and talked it was great to talk and listen I even got told off but it did no good she is my life

and if I can I will spoil my little angel my beautiful lady

She is a dream come true a godsend a blessing if you like but she is all mine I hope a dream that will come true

Garry Gosney

Day five arrived bill day payday broke again day...Thursday I spoke to my lady today it was great to hear her voice The voice of the lady I love so much and long to hear

The sounds of her laughter the sound of voice so sweet The touch of her arms in mine the body of a beautiful woman the lady I love so dear

Day six arrived she rang up and I spoke to the woman...Friday

The beautiful woman of my dreams she is truly a lady The only lady for me and the hardest part is being so far Far away from each other the pain of loneliness is great But her voice is the voice of an angel to me it was funny She was drunk and all she could do was laugh she was happy for the first time in a long time she was really happy

The saddest part I was not there to see and be with her but just hearing her happy made me happy too

I just hope her head is alright when my lady wakes up

Day seven arrived I just sit and wait waiting to see her...Saturday come home trying to talk to her every chance I get

That precious time together we call our own 5 mins or 10 mins or an hour or 2 it is our time to be together with the one we love It's so special no words can describe the feeling

that we have for each other or the love in my heart We steal each moment as our last and hold it dear waiting watching for the next fleeting moment we can be together

Day eight the time difference between us is great...Mystery Day It's my day her night my night her day very confusing

But my angel is worth every minute to me now and always Always will be this is the hardest day of all a day of any

A day of many hours the hours gained and the hours lost This is the days and nights rolled into one no past no future "But only now the time we cherish together the present time" "Our time to love and live with each other the time of now"

Controversial Dreams Wishes Hopes Lyrics

And My Heart Skips a Beat

The days are hot and lonely

But I close my eyes and picture you there

I feel the wind and can smell that oh so smell That soft sweet smell of your perfume

That only adds to your beauty And my heart skips a beat

The days are cold and lonely

I close my eyes and picture you there I feel your cold and open up my heart

Open up my heart to give you my warmth Darlin' you're cold but my heart is slowly warming up

And my heart skips a beat

The nights are long and lonely

But I look at the northern sky and see it's beauty I see the stars and the snow gently falling

All the time I'm thinking of you

The sparkle of the stars that you bring to my eyes The softness of your touch is like falling snow And my heart skips a beat

I thank you for coming into my life

I thank God for making you the sweetest part of life I thank Mother Nature for making you so special

I thank them both for they gave you a voice of an angel An angel they gave to me to cherish

I thank you God and Mother Nature And my heart skips a beat

Darlin'

Take my heart to cool your hot and lonely days Take my heart to warm your cold lonely days

Garry Gosney

Take my heart to comfort you during the lonely nights

God take my heart and use it to love and spread warmth as you do
And my heart skips a beat

Ti Amo...Darlin'... And my heart skips a beat

Controversial Dreams Wishes Hopes Lyrics

The Trucker's Run

It's getting to that special time of the year Sitting at home on the back porch Watching our children playing and calling

Calling mommy, daddy look at me, look at me We're just talking about everything and nothing It's nice be home for a few days or so

Then the silence is broken once more by the phone But no body wants to move and then I go

Darlin' that was the boss I have to go on the road again Darlin' I will be home as soon as I can

It's Christmas season kids I have to go and do the Christmas run The truck is loaded and I roll down the high ways and by ways Stopping long enough to unload and load and make a call

The phone is ring my heart starts pounding do I walk, do I run

I answer the phone "hi" I shout out to the kids daddy is on the phone They all say their hi's then leave, how are you darlin' how's things

I just called to say I love you and I'm ok and I miss you and the kids Darlin' don't cry I will be home as soon as I can

Darlin' do me just one little favor keep the front light on

With every truck that goes past my heart skips a beat and I stand still Is that him, then the phone rings and the silence is broken again

Do I run or do I walk and answer it with a "hi" just who could it be Is it the call I want or is it not, with a deep breath I say hello

Hi darlin' it's me then I hear a cry thank God your ok I miss you she said Sorry darlin' I could not call sooner but the truck is ok and doing fine I'm running a day late but I'm on the homeward bound run

I just called to say I love you and I'm ok and I miss you and the kids Darlin' do me just one little favor keep the front light on

Darlin' keep the home fires burning and that light on to guide me home

Garry Gosney

Not a moment goes by that I do not pray for a safe trip

Not a moment goes by that I do not ask God to watch over you and the kids Darlin' I don't know if I can make it up to you and kids but I will try God willing we will make this Christmas time a special time

But when God gave me you and the kids they were the most beautiful gift The best gift any one could ever want the gift of love

It's a great life the life on the road and coming home to the ones you love The people you meet along the way all brought together under one banner "the truckers run" the family that always grows in friendship

It's a code, it's a job, and it's a love, the truckers run

But the best part of the truckers run is the run home to little lady gal To the little lady gal the truckers wife and kids

Controversial Dreams Wishes Hopes Lyrics

My Little Trucker's Prayer

Dear God I am only little but this is my prayer God bless mommy and keep her safe

God her cooking is great but she fusses to much God but the rest can you give her patience

Dear God I am only little this is a hard one God bless the man I call daddy and keep him safe

God I don't see him much but when I do well Well he's funny, needs a shave, and always tired But God I love him to, but he can't cook to good God mommy is a better cook but

God daddy gives better horse rides and kicks the ball

But God that's not my prayer

You see God ! daddy drive a _ruck a big one

So Dear God please can take good care of the _ruck Keep it safe and keep it running so it can help daddy That way mommy gets the money to cook good

God it might help mommy to stop crying some times God if you can teach daddy to cook too :):):):)

God signing off now

God bless you God and keep you safe So you can help my family

God bless the truck (hey I got it right that time yippy) God bless mommy and daddy

I'm trying it again God just one more time God bless all the trucks and truckers out there In trucker land

God this is my little Truckers pray

Just you and me our little secret God bless you God

Merry Christmas God

I don't want anything God

Garry Gosney

Just mommy and daddy and the truck to be happy and home Home for Christmas

P.S.

Almost for got God your welcome to stay for Christmas We don't have much God, but we will share

I know I will I don't eat much

Controversial Dreams Wishes Hopes Lyrics

Special Time a Special Memory

Christmas time is here again special to some not so special to others But it dose not mean they will not celebrate it

This year is a different Christmas than all the rest "1" I have nothing to celebrate but it's not that

I don't believe, it's just I don't have or see my kids any more but that's another story

But I will always believe in the basic of Christmas "2" a lot of things have happened this year

to change the way Christmas is seen and celebrated In someway it's for the better in other ways it's worse But it is still Christmas no matter what

To all the families surviving the destruction of the trade center To all the families surviving the cleanup and any other tragedy To all the families surviving the wars were ever they may be To all the victims of these sad times

It is Christmas for every one something we should not forget

It's a special time of year a year of joy that ended in sadness It's a year none of us will but most definitely should never forget

We celebrate Christmas with our families and loved ones We share our hearts and our presents with family and friends

But this is a special time of year

A special time and a special year and a very special memory Would it hurt to have a minute silence at our Christmas breakfast Would it hurt to have a minute silence at our Christmas lunch Would it hurt to have a minute silence at our Christmas dinner Would it hurt to have a minute silence and a Christmas prayer

A Christmas prayer for all those that lost someone family or friend For all those serving in war were ever they may be

Garry Gosney

But most of for the innocent victim of crime the children

May this Christmas be the beginning of finding the true meaning again
May we celebrate it the way it was meant to be

Merry Christmas to all and a better New Year to everyone GOD BLESS YOU ALL

Controversial Dreams Wishes Hopes Lyrics

The Christmas Season

Christmas time is here again

A time to set up all the Christmas trees A time to put up the Christmas lights

A time to rejoice with family and friends A time to party and enjoy and rejoice

A time to sing a Christmas song or two A time for presents giving and receiving

A time to see the smiles on the children's faces A time to give thanks for all the joys of the season A time to share your home with family and friends

A time to remember just what charismas is all about A time to remember that a baby was born in a stable

A time to remember and reflect on the impact of a baby One tinny baby had on the world and why he was born Born to give us hope

Born to give us faith Born to give us himself Born to die for us

Born to show us how to love one another But most of all born to love us as equals

But at no time did he ever force himself onto us Born to be our friend if we let him

Christmas time is a time to open up our hearts Christmas time is a time to lend a hand Christmas time is a time to celebrate

Celebrate the birth of a love one a baby JESUS Celebrate it with the love in your heart Celebrate it with a prayer for all those less

Less fortunate then our self as God once did with the gift The gift of his son JESUS and the gift of love

Let us rejoice in what we have the love of family and friends And the love of God and knowing that he still cares

Garry Gosney

Merry Christmas One and All

Controversial Dreams Wishes Hopes Lyrics

It's Christmas Time

Put up the Christmas tree

Put on a happy face

Trim the tree with decorations

Put up the Christmas lights

The snow is falling brrrrr

It's Christmas time

Sing Christmas songs and drink eggnog Sing along to your favorite Christmas carols Deck the halls with holly and sing

Light the fire and roast marshmallows Turn the lights down low

Stuff the turkey to roast Put on the veggies and sing It's Christmas a time to rejoice

Set the table for all to see Put the presents under the tree Pack the stocking for all to see

Open up your hearts to family and friends Open the door to your heart and rejoice Rejoice for it is the time of giving

It is the time of sharing let us sing

Let us sing by the firelight and watch the snow

It's Christmas time every one

All children of to bed Santa is on his way Turn out the lights and sing a carol or two Sing for this is a special time of year

Sing songs of peace and joy sing of love Sing!! Sing!! Sing it's Christmas time

Jesus is born

Garry Gosney

Love For My Lady

The longing to hold the beautiful woman I love is hard The longing to hear my lady's voice a beautiful sound The longing to see my lady smile that beautiful smile The longing to see that look in her beautiful eyes

The look of a beautiful lady gal, the lady I love

The waiting game I heard was hard but my lady Is worth the wait, I dream of the days together

The day and night that will never end our togetherness These are the times that I am longing for

The times our hearts will never part

The times our love will never die but will get stronger These I hope will make our love stronger and stronger For the love for my lady is strong and hurts real bad This longing to have her by my side forever and a day

I LOVE YOU

Controversial Dreams Wishes Hopes Lyrics

My Love For You My LADY

I give you a real Red Rose to show you my Love

I give you a real White Rose to show you the purity of my Love I give you a real Yellow Rose for your hand in mine

I give you a real Pink Rose for a friendship so dear

I give you a imitation Red Rose to take with you where ever you go to remind you of my love for you

I give you a imitation White Rose to take with you where ever you go to remind you of the purity of my love for you

I give you a imitation Yellow Rose to take with you where ever you go to remind you my hand is holding your hand so dear and near

I give you an imitation Pink Rose to take with you where ever you go to remind you our friendship is real and dear

Wandering would an E Type Jaguar like to park beside a T Model Ford that needs restoring and a total revamp restoration job

Wandering if a beautiful Rose would like grow old beside a cactus

Missing is the heart I hold so dear yet so far and yet so near Missing is the hand I hold so dear yet so far and yet so near Missing is the lady I hold so dear yet so far and yet so near Missing is the love I hold so dear yet so far and yet so near Missing is the smile I long to see yet I hold them so dear Missing is the warm embrace of her arms around me Missing is the taste of her lips on mine yet I hold to them Missing these I cry a tear waiting for the day so far

Waiting for that day to come near and near that day so dear Waiting for my heart to bring our love one home my dear one to be Waiting waiting for that special day to come so I can hold her dear Waiting for that special moment to say I LOVE YOU so MUCH DEAR

There's a lot I would give you if I could but I have nothing to give But I would go with out just to make you happy as you make me Just being with me and by my side is all the happiness I need

Garry Gosney

No words or picture could say the way I feel about you right now The tears of sadness and joy you bring to me and my heart

But I can give you this much and say 7 words an hope they're enough I LOVE YOU WITH ALL MY HEART

Controversial Dreams Wishes Hopes Lyrics

The Spirits Watch

Darlin' hope you're ok Darlin' hope you had a good day

Darlin' hope you have a pleasant night Darlin' no matter were you are you're in my thoughts

Darlin' no matter what the time you're in my thoughts

The days become night and my heart is with you It saws like an eagle watching over you

It swims like a dolphin forever trying to protect The nights become days my heart is watching over you

Good morning darlin' ti amo where ever you are

Thousand miles apart yet you're in my thoughts Oceans apart yet you're in my heart

Darlin' may your dreams be good ones

Good night sweetheart ti amo darlin' where ever you are

May the spirit of the eagle bring you protection May the spirit of the dolphin bring peace calm

May the spirit of my heart hold you when you sleep May the spirit of my heart be at your when your awake May the spirit of the white dove bring everlasting comfort

Darlin' may God's angels guide you in what ever you do Follow and listen to your heart for hearts do talk

The heart talks and love listens and watches over you

Garry Gosney

Heavens Smiling Down Me

Sitting here listening to my favorite songs Thinking of what can I give a beautiful woman But there is a catch I am poor and

She is so beautiful She is so special to me

She is my friend, my better half, and much much more All I can think of is my love for you and what you do to me

Thinking off what you really mean to me

It was no accident me finding you Someone had a hand in it, long before ever knew

Now I just can't believe your in my life Heavens smiling down me, as I look at you tonight

I tip my hat, to the keeper of stars

He sure knew what he was doing when he joined these two hearts I hold everything, when I hold you in my arms and I've got all I'll ever need thanks to the Keeper of the Stars

Soft moonlight on your face, oh how you shine

It takes my breath away, just to look into your eyes

All I can think of is how beautiful you are in your own way All I can think off how you make me feel inside

Here is a copy of sticker I brought it kinda said it all

B = Beautiful I = Intelligent T = Talented C = Charming

H = Horny

This in many many ways made me love you just the way you are One word that's all you said

Something in your voice caused me

To turned my head, your smile

Just captured you and me were in my future

Controversial Dreams Wishes Hopes Lyrics

Far as I could see and I don't know how it happened But it happens still, you ask me if I love you

If I always will...Well... You had me from "Hello"

I felt love start to grow, the moment that I looked into your eyes You won me, it was over from the start

You completely stole my heart and now you won't let go

I never even had a chance you know you had me from "Hello"

All I could think off is what could I possibly have to give you All I have is me and that's all

All I have is nothing but my love for you All I can think off is does she feel the same All I can think off will she like what I have Thousands off miles apart but my love is real

Our love is unconditional, we knew it from the start I see it in your eyes, you can feel it in my heart

From here on after lets stay the way we are right now And share all love and laughter that a lifetime will allow I cross my heart and promise to

Give all I've got to give to make all your dreams come true In all the world you'll never find a love as true as mine Darlin' I give you the only thing I can give my

"Love and my heart" for that is all I have to give

Garry Gosney

The True Beauty

I sit and think of things that might have been I think of the good times we shared together I think of the bad times we shared together But most of all I think of the love we shared You opened up my heart to love

But most of all you showed me the real you You taught me to see with my heart

You gave me hope to believe in love of the heart You showed me everything was possible

If you believe in God

Well through you I found faith, hope in God

I asked and God gave me you to love as only I can I asked for a plain woman on the outside

I asked for a pretty woman on the inside But I had no idea just how beautiful you are

I see a rose and all I can do is think of you

I see a carnation and I think of your soft touch Then all I can think of how much time God put in To making you so beautiful in everyway possible

Not a day goes by I do not thank God for making you

Every day I thank God for putting you into my life I thank God for showing my heart how to love again

But most of all I pray that he keeps you safe To me you are plain yet oh so beautiful

But the true beauty is in knowing and loving you

Darlin'

I pray that God will make your day pleasant

May all you dreams and wishes come true I give you my heart and

Controversial Dreams Wishes Hopes Lyrics

love to comfort you

I pray that God will watch over you, keep you safe

Ti Amo

Garry Gosney

So Many Things

So many things I want to say So many things I want to do So many things I want to give

So many things I can never do or give or say

I want to be able to take away your pain I want to give you everything you deserve I want to say what you really mean to me

A thousand tears I shed for these things I not do

Darlin' I'm sorry I can not take your pain away I'm sorry I can give you what you deserve I'm sorry I don't know the right works say

A thousand more because I don't have the power

Darlin' you're always in my prayers Darlin' all I can give you is my love and my heart

Darlin' you make so proud to be part of you

A thousand tears I cry for the joy you bring to me

I pray that God can take your pain away I pray that God will keep you healthy

I pray that God will keep our love strong

I pray that God will help in giving what you deserve Most of all I pray that what I have to give is enough An imperfect me, nothing special, just plain old me

Controversial Dreams Wishes Hopes Lyrics

Hours That Seem to Never End

The days and night are long The hours seem to never end I see you everywhere I go

I see you in everything I do I feel your pain

But it don't matter to you You ask me to write

You say you will answer but you never do Each day is getting harder and harder

Just wandering if she is for real

Or is she a fake like the rest off them Just wandering what game is she playing She talks but it's as though she says nothing

Her interests seem to be else were

It's as though to you I do not exist anymore

So many times I try to say what you mean to me The hours seem to never end

Each hour seems like a day Each day seems like a week

But to you it's as though I do not exist anymore

Garry Gosney

The Ocean Has My Heart

Looking out over the ocean

Just watching the waves lap the shore Thinking just were does it start and finish I close my eyes and listen to the sounds

To the sounds of the ocean as it laps the shore I listen to the waves coming and going

I listen to the sounds of your voice

I close my eyes and picture you there with me Walking hand in hand on the waters edge

I hear you laugh and I see you smile Then I wake and find it was only a dream

I wipe the tears from eyes but it does not help My heart is still heavy for it's not free

It's in love with you an ocean apart I set it free only to see it swim to you It drifts with the tide in to your heart

But the tears keep flowing drop after drop One drop for I love you, one drop for I'm a fool One drop for you have my heart, drop by drop I wipe the tears from eyes but it does not help

For the ocean has my heart taking it straight to you I close my eyes and picture you there with me Walking hand in hand on the waters edge

Controversial Dreams Wishes Hopes Lyrics

Nothing Can Mend

To talk about something who or what does it help But the funny thing is it don't help nothing does No matter which way I look at it nothing helps. his friend says:

It doesn't help to talk about it? he says:

It might help others understand me but it don't help me his friend says:

You're right your situation is still the same he says:

Not easy hey his friend says:

But you have someone to share your pain with he says:

Yep but I still have to carry the burden and the load his friend says:

yes he says:

That's why I bury things or kill them off the way I do I have done it all my life

his friend says:

But Garry think of the love you're stopping from getting in he says:

I am and I did and I got screwed

I lost the only things I ever cared about his friend says:

I just read your last page and your heart is truly broken That has to be very tough

And I don't know what you are feeling you're right he says:

What page is that his friend says:

The Ocean Has My Heart

All I can say is that I pray to God that you will learn to love a gain he says:

Well pray I stop crying his friend says:

Garry Gosney

That is my prayer for you too dear friend he says:

I'm sick of crying myself to sleep and waking up crying his friend says:

You are lonely, are you crying now he says:

I'm ok, what do u think his friend says:

Yes he says:

Xmas time // no kids // my sons birthday // what do u think he says:

I only have my music his friend says:

I think you are in pain and no pain is greater than the loss of your children

he says:

Thanks, but I will bury it in time I will put it all to rest

I did the same when I was boarding school I will do it again his friend says:

Where do you find the room to bury all the hurt you have carried all your life

he says:

It's part of my heart his friend says:

You have carried more than your share for sure he says:

Yep you can say that his friend says:

My friend you have let me see a side of you this morning

That has broke my heart and I hope that someday Those pieces of your heart will be put back together

And empty of all the things you have been burying all these years

The truth is that will never happen

Not while I am alive there is nothing that can take away the feeling inside

Controversial Dreams Wishes Hopes Lyrics

Nothing can mend the damage that is already done Nothing can mend the time that has been stolen or lost Friends are great to have while they are around you

But when they go home you are the only one left to fix the problem

They say love can mend a broken heart yep to a point that is true But at no time do the scares ever go away or fade

There are only 2 things in life you can gamble on and win every single time

1 = you were born alone…2 = you die alone… Anything else along the way is just a driving force

Each scar a reminder and with a story but most of them will never get told

They just get killed of and buried deep within your heart as a reminder

A reminder of all thing past and things to come A dream of the past or a dream of the future It's still a dream of a scared heart

Garry Gosney

The Ones in Power

The AUSTRALIAN Prime Minister John Howard has defended Governor-General Peter Hollingworth ex (arch bishop) amid claims he covered up sexual abuse allegations at

a second Queensland Anglican school as quoted on channel 9 news 21 dec 2001

Rape of a child is the worse there is 90 % of is done by those in power

But it's not the rape that hurts so much

It's the fact that it was done by the ones in power Done by ones that you should have trusted

And that no-one believes you when your under 13 In the 60,s to late 80,s it's was never spoken off If it was just who could you get to believe you

Believe you after all these years have past Just who will believe you

Who do you turn to what do you say Better still how do you say it

When the ones involved are dead or to old to care The church don't care they never did

They deny it now that it happened and they did it then So just what do you do ! you spend your life burying it You berry it 30 to 38 years go only to have it resurface But it still dose no good there's still no one you can trust How can you trust anyone in power again

When everyone in power always abuse it in one way or another Politicians feather their own nest

And pass legislation to rip of people on disability pensioners Or from any pensioner or people in need so just who can you trust They are quick to pass the buck down the line

So they never have to take responsibility for what there staff do Just were is the buck passing going to stop and responsibility start

Controversial Dreams Wishes Hopes Lyrics

Everyone in power wants to sweep it under the carpet

...it never happened...But it's mostly the ones in power doing the damage The damage being they deny and don't want to know what there staff are doing

Just when will the governments stand up and say no more child rape Just when will they admit they play a big part in all child rape

Past and future

Stop hiding behind the door open it and see the people you trust The ones that we should but never can and never will

Just when will the stealing stop Just when will the rape stop

Just when will psychological rape stop

Just how many times do we have to relive the memories? The memories that we want to forget and leave buried When we are all dead

Just when will you take a stand and say enough is enough

Marry CHRISTMAS

Garry Gosney

A Season to Remember

Hi it's Christmas time once again A time to rejoice

A time for sharing A time to forgive

A time for showing love towards each other

A time to remember the true meaning of Christmas

The year has passed

To some it was a kind year To some it was a cruel year

But what ever happened with the year Now is the festive time

Time to celebrate with family and friends A time to reflection the year pasted

A time to bring joy to those with a saddened heart

A time to rejoice the Christ is born

A time for the northern star to celebrate A time for the southern star to celebrate

Time for each star to rejoice an watch over each other A time to comfort those in need

It's Christmas time once again

A time to prayer for peace and good will A time that should be so special to us all

A time to thank god for our friends and family A time to open up our hearts to those in need

A time to lend an ear A time to give your heart

A time to open your hand

A time to share a prayer with others

A time to reflect of the love that God gave us In the birth of his son Jesus on this special day

Controversial Dreams Wishes Hopes Lyrics

Season Greetings God bless you one and all
For you make this festive season A season to remember
Merry Christmas and Happy New Year

Garry Gosney

The Price Is the Same

Over the last 4 yrs or so I have learnt a lot Learnt that 95% of all people on the net are fake They say one thing and totally mean another

The sad part is that none of them are true to them selves All they want is for you to give and give and give

The best part is now I can take it or leave it

Take it with a grain of salt a touch of pepper an arsenic But that is the same as life in general

You care for someone but it is always a one way street You care but they never do unless they can get something

It's all a game to them to see just how far they can go Just how much will you give to them before you wake up They say they want love for love but what they really want

Real want is everything you can give them

So long as they don't have to give you anything in return

They say material things don't matter but the truth is they do The more you have and the better it is the better the chances Better the chances you have with them

Everything is based on How much you make How much you got How much you own And what you own

They do not want to work as an equal to make love work

Once that is all sorted out then they look at you and compare Will I, can I, should I, what's in it for me, what can I get

What do I need, then they look some more and compare some more We all compare that is true but mostly for personal reason

Mostly because of the way we're treated before by our ex's But the saddest part is the honesty is gone out of love for love It's now lets see what can I get now

Controversial Dreams Wishes Hopes Lyrics

What do I want later on down the track Just how much is it worth to me

Everything has a price on it for love for love is gone Replaced by love you but I want more now what can you give me But I want love for love to but I want more and all you can give

I wander just when will they wake up to themselves Love for love has no price, richer or poorer the price is the same

It's free and it's from the heart

Garry Gosney

53 State Little America

Today was funny it started with a phone call

A call from the American consulate in Sydney 61 - 2 - 93739176 He was the most arrogant, naive, rude person God put on the earth

I though my EX WIFE was but he left her for dead

I have ever met in 45 yrs and he could hardly speak english I thought I learnt a lot driving taxis in 8yrs

But no...I met him on the phone today

He had no common sense at all and no logic and was so bloody rude I could only think what is the American government employing

But a friend came up with a great excuse for him

The American government doesn't trust their employees to handle money I could only wonder at the stupidity off it all

There was no mention of ever paying money into the Australian Post Office There was no mention of having to send a self addressed return envelope All I could think off was that America was cutting back on website space And cutting back one writing envelopes with names and address on and stamps

I could no help wandering just how much America is going broke Are they the next country to go into bankruptcy

By employing people that can't read and rite enough to fill out an envelope

And lick a stamp...We are the 53 State of America...Yet we are treated like like trash

They ask our government to fight beside them in war

But they treat the Australian Citizen as scum, second class, third rate I thought governments trusted there employees to handle cash and bank it ect etc

Controversial Dreams Wishes Hopes Lyrics

But nope I learnt today they don't...I don't know weather to laugh or cry I checked the web site twice today both times with a friend and no were No were on the site it says anything about a self addressed envelope No were on the site it says anything about paying at the Australian

Post Office

And in the emails we got back there was no mention off them either and we asked

We even rang the American Embassy in Canberra and they never knew of it either

Just what happened to common sense that the American Government can not accept

Except a bank cheques !! They can not even accept travelers cheques !! or cash

They expect that we should be able to read the fine print when there isn't any

And they want us to read there minds This is the 53 State Little America

We are Australians we like things plain and simple things Slow and easy, what don't get done today will tomorrow, you do

not get paid

Get paid to kill yourself for stupidity sake.

You get paid for using common sense and logic

You get paid for trying your best to do your job right the first time not 10 times later

My friend said the law is the law and rules are rules

If they were to cover every situation no one would ever be able to learn it all

Well to an extent that is true...BUT

What happened to common sense !! logic !! and trying to understand

Garry Gosney

people

Understand people that are trying to do the rite thing

But do not understand the legal paper work or read peoples minds Is this the way society has gone the average people get treated like scum

You ask for help because you don't fully understand only to get Treated like scum a second rate citizen

I want to thank that American government employee from the bottom of my heart

For making me fell like scum a second rate citizen

I hope the American public treats people with a lot more respect Than their government employees do. I am human and I make mistakes

And I will make mistakes in the states you can bank on it

But I will watch and learn and hopefully it turns out ok, I'm Not Perfect Because I ask for common sense and logic to prevail

I can bet they will stop my visa or do everything in their power to stop it But I'm Just a Pawn in life so I can not expect to be treated with respect As I am poor.

But I hope the American government will see the logic in what I say At No Time do I blame the Government

I Just Would like the people working there think of the people that Don't and try to help them understand a bit more so we can do the right thing by you all

Controversial Dreams Wishes Hopes Lyrics

Wanted One Beautiful Imperfection

Why is love so hard to find

What makes us do things that we know is wrong They say the heart talk and love listens

Christmas time is the worse time for me In more ways than one I miss my children

But there is nothing I can do to fix the problem I have tried but did no good it's hard to explain And not many if any will ever understand

I went in to a few adult rooms I don't normally go And the saddest thing is I saw a lot

A lot of woman each Beautiful in the own way They were stripping to show everyone their assets All in the name of finding someone to except them Except them and approve of what they have to offer

The men were even doing the same

I just could not understand why the need Need to go that far

I was ashamed and yet proud to see what I saw The body is beautiful each in their own way But it's not the body that is beautiful

It's not the size of what we do or do not have It's the inner beauty the gift to see from within

Why is love so hard to find

What makes us do things that we know is wrong They say the heart talk and love listens

Will we ever see the beauty of the heart from within Will we ever feel the beauty from within

Well we ever be excepted for the body we have The gift of love is loving from within

The gift of love is excepting each others beauty The beauty of imperfection is Gods creation Wanted one good heart

Garry Gosney

Wanted one beautiful heart

Wanted one imperfect body with a beautiful heart to love W A N T ED

Controversial Dreams Wishes Hopes Lyrics

Ordinary Man Dreams

I see your picture I hear your voice A voice so special A voice so rare

A voice that makes me feel special Just the way you talk and laugh

You give me hope You make me feel special

You make feel like I can do anything You make a plain man feel special Why I will never know

The special one is you and you alone For you make me feel like a king Your voice, your smile, your laugh For the way you make me feel

You are the special one

For you're special ever so special to me For you give this ordinary man hope You're a wish and a dream come true An ordinary mans dream come true

Garry Gosney

Ti Amo My Friend

Just what is beauty ???

I see you cry

But it never stops the way I feel I see you laugh

But it never stops the way I feel I see you play

But it never stops the way I feel I see you work

But it never stops the way I feel I see you in the good times

But it never stops the way I feel I see you in the bad times

But it never stops the way I feel I see you in the first of light

But it never stops the way I feel I see you at the dark of night But it never stops the way I feel I see you in the moonlight

But it never stops the way I feel I see you glow amongst the stars But it never stops the way I feel Just what is beauty I wonder

The beauty is knowing you are near But it never stops the way I feel

The beauty is knowing your a pain But it never stops the way I feel

The beauty is knowing you except me for the pain I am

But it never stops the way I feel The beauty of life is loving you Beauty is having you for my friend Ti Amo My Friend

Controversial Dreams Wishes Hopes Lyrics

Hearts Do Talk If You Believe

I look outside into the dark of night

I see the moon smiling and the stars dancing I hear the night owls sing through the trees

And all I can do is marvel at the work that was done God and Mother Nature sure made them beautiful

I close my eyes and listen to my country music

I hear nature's sounds blending in with my music But at the same time all I can do is think of you

I just can't help but think of there most beautiful Most beautiful creation of all

If a picture can say a thousand words I know it will not do you justice

For there are no words to describe the way you make me feel I can only hope that our hearts will talk as one

Just how do you tell a beautiful imperfection you care

Just what words would you use or could you use Just how do you tell a scared heart it is beautiful

Just how do you tell an imperfection that they are beautiful A thousand tears I cry for there is no answers

I can only hope that my heart will talk to yours

I close my eyes and listen to the sounds of the music play I wipe away a tear or two for you have my heart

I wipe away a few more for I can not be with you as one But how do you tell Gods most beautiful creation you care

How do you thank Mother Nature for giving you an imperfection

I just hope and pray that someday our hearts will talk

I just hope and pray that someday our dreams will come true I can only pray the my heart will find the right words to say

Garry Gosney

I close my eyes and I can see through this scared heart your beauty A scared heart that wants to talk and hope that someday love listens

Controversial Dreams Wishes Hopes Lyrics

A Person's Word of Trust

Just why is the people you are suppose to trust always trying to Why is it they are always trying to lie to you

Just why is it they are always trying to steal of you

One thing was driven home today and that is you can trust no one You hire a solicitor to help you only to find they have lied to you You hire them only to find out they are steeling of you

And the best part is they can get away with it for they make the law Make it and twist it to suit themselves when and were they want to

The owner says one thing and you shake on it only to find he lied to you Only to find that he says one thing to your face and his staff steal from you All under the system we are suppose to call the law

Yep they are right it is the law

A law unto them self just like the ones the **POLITICIANS** *and doctors hide under*

And never the two shell meet for it's the law they can use for whatever means

The means to lie to you, the means to steal of off you, what happened

What happened to a person's word of trust

The mafia has more loyalty and honesty then any one will ever know At least you have two choices live or die

You have your solicitor lying and stealing of you You have the doctors saying one thing to your face

You have the **POLITICIANS** *lying to you and stealing from you And they all say the opposite when you're gone*

Just so long as they feather their own nest they don't care

The ones that you should trust you can't

They just kill you slowly piece by piece until your a living corps Numb

Garry Gosney

all over, and nothing left, no respect or dignity left

They want it all so just who can you trust

Just what will it take to trust again

Just what will it take "John Hutchinson" to get ones self respect back

Just what will it take "Sue Watts" to get ones dignity back

You have done a good job in trying to kill them off

Just so you can add the pieces together we agreed 23,500 cash in hand After all government medical and government charges were taken out

$9,000.oo

+$14,500.oo

=$23,500.oo

Not a penny more or a penny less john

NOT $9,000.oo

+ $12,278.10

= $21,278.10

No matter which way you slice it or dice it…it is not

NOT $23,500.oo as agreed in words by you "John" and over a hand shank But I am not lawyer or a solicitor only a pensioner

I take people at their word

But know I know I can never do that again thanks to you "John and Sue" You both have made sure that anyone that is suppose to help people

I do say, "suppose to" can never be trusted or recommended to anyone As they only lie to you and steal from you

Sue you and have done everything power not to work on this case As far as work goes you have not done one thing I have asked of you As far as that goes you have not done a honest days work on this case

You or the owner…you have lied…and tried to avoid every thing you

Controversial Dreams Wishes Hopes Lyrics

could

You both are a disgrace to your country and to your profession You should not be allowed to practice law or have anything to do with again And I know you will continue to avoid paying me my 23,500...as you

avoided

Avoided everything else I have asked to be done by your firm

Thanks for driving home the only one that you can trust is your enemy

Not the one you pay to help you.

It's a shame I can not recommend a fellow human or a company To use your services

It will be a cold day in hell before I can Recommend your firm to the DEAD

Like going behind my back to my friend it won't help you

But if you want to go to court please do and I will open the case up About your incompetence right from day one as a solicitor

So when your ready I am to

Lets open this case up to the media lets show how the law rips off pensioners

Sue your famous words "your not worth that much

"you will never get that much" "your not worth it"

Garry Gosney

Torn Between

Torn between two minds Torn between two loves Torn between a dream Torn between a wish Torn between a hope

Torn between two minds One to stay and one to go

To stay for the family I don't see Or to go and try to start a new one Torn between my mind and my heart

Torn between two loves The love I have for my children

The love for my mother and children Or the love I have inside for a country Torn between my mind and my love

Torn between a dream

A dream to have something to call my own A dream to leave something for my children Is it a dream or is it a dream your heart makes

Torn between a dream and my heart

Torn between a wish

A wish for a peace and happiness A wish to be accepted for who I am Torn between a wish to find me Torn between a wish and my mind

Torn between a hope

A hope for a better future in a land I love

A hope I can find my heart and bring it home A hope that some day I will have my children A hope that God will someday understand me A hope that someday we will be as one in love A hope that someday we will be as one in heart

A simple man with a simple dream and a simple wish Will this country boy ever find a home

torn between two loves, two minds and a dream Just what will it take to make two torn loves as one Just what will it take to make two torn hearts as one God maybe someday you will repair this torn heart

Controversial Dreams Wishes Hopes Lyrics

From Somewhere to Nowhere to Somewhere

Yesterday I finally found the nerve I was missing The nerve to commit to putting an end to a life

And the nerve to commit to trying to start a new one

There is still only one question to be asked "is it the right move"

There is only one answer

"I will find out the answer on my death bed" If any of my kids show up

But until then I will never know I can only hope

The time has come to bury what has to be buried The time has come to sever this life and move on The waiting for the word that could change things But the word did not come

Not a word since the 1 June 1998 Not a word since the 7 January 2002 NOT a THING

The hardest part was done yesterday Yesterday I finally found the nerve I was missing

The nerve to commit to putting an end to a life And the nerve to commit to trying to start a new one

I finally brought my ticket from nowhere to somewhere Or did I buy it from somewhere to nowhere

That is the million dollar question

It's hard to explain it's like a heavy load has gone But at the same a new one has taken it's place

I can't ask you to understand something you never will Yesterday a life has died and cannot be revived

Today a life has started a new

But for the better or for good I doubt if I will ever Will ever find out in this lifetime

I lost my kids in 1998

Garry Gosney

Only to permanently loose them again on 21 Feb. 2001 When their mother showed a letter stating

I was in West Australia the letter the courts can not find Now I loose them for the last time 22 January 2002

They loose me again just to get my computer to keep in touch If they ever do it is their choice it was never mine

All I hope for is a new start somewhere but where If not all I can say it was never meant to be

The story of my life

Controversial Dreams Wishes Hopes Lyrics

The True Wild Flower of Life

"hold me close in your embrace" "love me face to face an heart to heart"

Great words for someone to live and love by

I can give you a rose to show I love you

I can give a carnation to show just how much I care I can give you a wildflower

They grow wild in the countryside but they add the beauty They add their own beauty to the countryside

They add a special kind of beauty the kind the heart makes

The heart loves freely just as the wildflowers grow freely The true beauty is in the free just as it was meant to be You can not tie a heart down but if it's free it will stay

The wildflowers have a special kind of beauty wild and free Wild an free but oh so so beautiful to the eye

They are a delight to the eye and so beautiful to hold So wild and free and yet so soft and delicate to touch I can give you a rose to show I love you

I can give a carnation to show just how much I care I can give you a wildflower for it's free

I give you my heart for it's free I give you my love as it's free

For you are as beautiful as a wild flower

For you have a beautiful heart that I do not want to tame So wild and so free and so beautiful to the holder

A true gift from God and so beautiful like nature intended For YOU are the true WILDFLOWER of life

Garry Gosney

My Driving Force

Just how many times and ways do we live in the past Must it always be there to haunt us

Or is it the driving force behind our heart

Just what make the heart so strong and yet so weak So strong love can over come almost anything

So strong yet our heart can be as soft and gentle as a lamb So strong that a baby can turn your heart into putty

So strong that death make you weak as the tears running down you face

Yet through all life's ups and downs our hearts remain torn Torn but scared for life but it's how we use it that makes a difference

Do we or can we turn all hated into a driving force for the better Better still will we ever find that missing heart that missing link Or will our hearts forever search the heartlands forever and a day

Just what is the driving force behind the heart Where does that driving force come from

We see and hear about so much destruction and it makes a grown man cry

We see and hear about some small miracle like a birth of a baby That funny little bundle of joy that can melt the strongest of hearts

Just what is the driving force that keeps us going

Just what is the driving force that makes our heart keep beating Just what is the driving force that's makes our love so strong yet so weak

Just what is the hold that you have over me that cannot be broken

Is it you that is my driving force that light ever so bright light Is it the smile and the warmth of your soft touch

Just what is your heart doing to mine

Controversial Dreams Wishes Hopes Lyrics

Just what power if any does love have over the heart

Maybe someday God will reveal what he has planed But until then I will just have to follow my heart

Garry Gosney

While I Have a Today

Tonight I celebrate my love with you Today I celebrate my love with you

I cannot promise for the future For yesterday is yesterday

For today is today

And tomorrow is always today

But while I have a today you will always have my heart

Yesterday is past and gone and sometimes forgotten But my love was real then as it is now but never forgotten

Today I love you just as I did yesterday Today you are just as special as yesterday

Tomorrow if God willing will be just as beautiful

Yesterday and today and tomorrow are just days Just days like the past, present and future

That only mean the time I have known you is real I can only love you for today and today is real

Just as a rose is beautiful and a gift from God Just as a carnation is soft and a gift from God

Just as a butterfly is so gentle and a gift from God The true gift from God is knowing and loving you for you

The beauty of a rose, the softness of the carnation The gentleness of a butterfly can only enhance the best The best gift God and Mother Nature could ever create

For you darlin' are true beauty of all Gods creations

And to that I must thank them both from the bottom of my heart

Tonight I celebrate my love with you Today I celebrate my love with you

I can not promise for the future For yesterday is yesterday

Controversial Dreams Wishes Hopes Lyrics

For today is today

And tomorrow is always today

But while I have a today you will always have my heart While I have a today you will always be a special part of me

Garry Gosney

Voice That Has Painted a Picture

The way you make feel tonight Is more then word can say

Because when the heart talks love listens

Just how many times have I heard that said

I guess more than I can count or care to remember I close my eyes and listen to the voice of an angel Just what's in that voice that has painted a picture

Painted a picture beautiful woman

Some may say nothing special to look at well that maybe But to me she is special with a heart of gold yet poor

She is poor yet she is beautiful in voice and heart She make you feel special just by her voice

Just what's in her voice that makes you want to be together To be together and to grow old as one in love

They say when hearts talk love listen

They for got to say that heart picks the perfect moment They for got to say that heart picks out the true beauty

They say the eyes are the window to the soul and see all Well mine are black and are to deep to see into

But my heart sees what I need to see and need to hear They say the heart hears every sound two lovers make

Maybe someday I will find out

If you ever feeling like loving me again the door is open My heart is always open and thinking just what would it What would it be like to grow old with you in my arms That oh so special voice that has painted a picture

In my heart

Controversial Dreams Wishes Hopes Lyrics

My Door Is Always Wide Open

I look at the stars and all they do is amaze me I see them dancing against the dark of night

But I look into your eyes and I see the real beauty This is the moment for this is the time I will cherish This one last time just how special you will always be A cherished moment in time that can never be erased A cherished moment that will live forever and ever

The way you make feel tonight is more then word can say No matter what I say can take way the pain and the hurt

Much as I want to I can not take away the pain for it's too great

Anytime with you was perfect even when we had our differences But I always loved you and always will my way it's all I know Imperfect as it maybe, but I never said I was perfect

But the best times I had was watching you play and laugh Best time was holding you in my arms whenever you wanted it But now it's never to be any more

I look at the southern stars and all I see is you And I hope that someday you will find me again

We can not pick up the pieces were we left off or repair it But hopefully someday we can start over again

If you ever feel like needing someone Or ever feel like loving me again

My door is always wide open for you For you are oh so so special to me

Garry Gosney

The Voice of Beauty

All I can think of is just how much you mean to me I hear your voice and marvel at the sounds of beauty

Laying here thinking just what would it be like

Be like to see you walking towards me for the first time Be like to just hold you in my arms for the very first time

Just wandering what words do I or can I say if any at all How can you show something which is lost deep within darkness

They say the eyes are the light and the way to your heart What if there is no light but only just a flicker in the distant

Just wandering will she understand and except or just turn around

All I can think of is what you mean to me Just what is it that you see

See in a no-body, a no-body with nothing to offer you

A thousand tears I shed because you deserve far more than me A nobody with a dream and in love with a plain but beautiful lady

Just what would it be like to see for the first time

Just what would be like to hold you and walk side by side Just what can I say to improve on the most perfect moment time

Improve on the gift from God and Mother Nature and Father Time

All I can think of is just how much you mean to me I hear your voice and marvel at the sounds of beauty

Laying here thinking just what would it be like

Is it a dream come true or what will it take to make the dream real I close my eyes and hear your voice

so plain but oh so ever so beautiful as only Mother Nature intended

Controversial Dreams Wishes Hopes Lyrics

An Angel in Disguise

She wants to be wanted She knows when she's needed

Just what would it take to love you Just what can this poor heart give you

Darlin' you say I make you happy You say I make your heart dance and sing

Darlin' if that is true then I am happy Darlin' if that is true then why do you cry

Darlin' you say I make you happy

But do you really know what you do to me You give a poor heart hope

You give warmth and love when needed

Darlin' I have 3 angels in my life One is my best friend

One is my daughter

And one is a lady so rare oh so rare

I asked God for a miracle

I asked Mother Nature to make her plain But Darlin' they stuffed my order up big time

They sent me an angel in disguise

An angel in the shape of a beautiful imperfection A woman more pretty then I could ever imagine Ever imagine or ever hope for a dream come true An angel in the shape of a beautiful lady gal

I can't promise moonlight and romance I can't promise fame and riches

But I can promise rags and love

But all I can really do is promise to try my best For you are the best and a true gift from God An angel in disguise

Garry Gosney

My Perfect Night

Darlin' just what would a perfect night be Well I just don't know for you're a dream come true

You are the best part of me a true gift

A perfect night is any night with you

A sunset by the lake or a sunset by a waterfall A sunset by the beach or a sunset in the gardens

A sunset picnic dinner for two and a walk with you

Just to name a few a perfect night with natures backdrop But they only add to the true beauty of the lady

The lady who stole my heart and who made this night This night so special and such a wonderful night

Denim & lace and a white rose for purity A candle light dinner and a red rose for love

A walk in the park and a yellow rose for your hand Soft music and a carnation to soften the stars

These are just some of the things that make up a perfect night Darlin' you are the perfect night you bring joy to my heart Happy valentines day darlin' this is your day darlin'

This is your special day for you bring me so much happiness

Just loving you is enough for you are my perfect night For you are a delight to hold and you make any day perfect

For you are my perfect night

Controversial Dreams Wishes Hopes Lyrics

Garry Gosney

Beautiful Music

I don't know what you did to my heart...

I don't know how or what you used to captured it... But you did something to my heart...

How, when, where, why, I will never know... Darlin' I don't want to know for you are the light... You are the gift sent down from God...

Darlin' you are the second most precious gift... I have ever had the pleasure to hold...

Darlin' my kids are first

But you are the one with my heart to keep... For you are my light and the true beauty...

You are the best part of me . a dream come true...

I am blessed and honored that you are going to marry me... But most of all I am honored for you gave me the chance to love you...

And I love loving you...

Darlin' you play such beautiful music for my heart...

I love you dear lady...

Controversial Dreams Wishes Hopes Lyrics

Look at You Girl

I look at you girl And all I can do is think

Thinking of just what you see in me

I see the hope and love you give to me I see the love that we shared

But all the time I can't think of why

I look up into the dark of night

I see the stars and wander at there beauty Each beautiful star to a lonely heart

Just looking and thinking into the dark of night Thinking at the beautiful sites god gave us Thinking just what star did I wish on to find you

I look at you girl and all I can do is think Thinking of just what you see in me

A ordinary male with an attitude But still in love with you

I pray every day and night that its not a dream I see the dark of night and marvel at the stars

I pray that it would rain so you can not see me cry

A thousand tears I shed for you for my love is real A thousand more I shed for I can't be with you

I pray that it will rain so it will cover up my tears

I asked God what did I ever do to deserve you in my life Just what is it he wants from me in return

But I can only thank him for bringing you into my life

I look at you girl and all I can do is think Thinking of just what you see in me I who have nothing

All I can think of is just how you make feel in side All I want to do is hold you and love you

Garry Gosney

Love you my way forever

Controversial Dreams Wishes Hopes Lyrics

Dancing to the Call

The moon is full

A perfect backdrop against the dark of night The stars are dancing their dance of dances A night waltz so beautiful so see

The music is so peaceful and graceful to hear

The moon is full and shines so beautiful

It lights up the night skies to show their beauty The beauty of the clouds dancing their dance The meeting of the southern and northern clouds The meeting of the northern and southern stars

All dancing to the call dancing to the call of time Dancing to the call of the heart

Will these two ever meet and join as one

Just how will the northern star except a southern cloud Can they shine and comfort each other as one

Soft lights and music and a perfect backdrop Nature at its best the comfort and beauty of the clouds The beauty the stars all dancing to the call of the heart

Just thinking will I find my cloud for comfort Just thinking will I find my shining star

I see the stars dancing in the dark of night to the call And all I can do is think of you and happy you make me feel

I see the stars resting in the comfort of the clouds And all I do is think of the comfort and joy you bring me

Just what will the perfect backdrop be to the call Dancing to the call of the heart

Garry Gosney

Two Strangers with One Heart

Just what is it like to be a stranger Well now I know first hand

It's a funny feeling in a lot of ways Strange and yet so formula in a lot of ways to

Coming to a new land is not easy

But when you're following a dream it's harder still Hard because you have no home or place to belong Hard because you have lived there all your life

Hard when you're a stranger in the night Like two stars in the dark of night never touching

Just wandering if they belong or have a home Just drifting with the flow wherever it may lead

Two countries, two hearts, two loves, two people Will the strangers ever untie and become as one Will they bridge the gap of time and distance They say the heart don't lie I just hope that's true

Just what is it that makes a heart love Love and live somewhere else while you drift

They say hearts can live and love as one

Until the day they can united the bodies as one in love

Two strangers in love living alone but loving as one Two countries, two hearts, two loves, two people Strangers they maybe but married by heart

Two heart married and living as one in love

Controversial Dreams Wishes Hopes Lyrics

Aged Before Your Time

I see you in my heart aged but still beautiful I see just how much you have aged

In the time we shared and loved

But I have seen just how much you have grown old Grown old before your time and I cry a thousand tears

I saw the true beauty in your eyes

I saw the beauty that made me love you

The times are hard and made you age before your time But you have kept the best part of you beautiful

The best part of you is you

The best is the gift you share with others You share your heart and your love

A gift which God could only give to you Just what is it that makes you so special You age for time is cruel to you

You work to make things work out

I can not pity you for you are proud

I can not envy you for you ask for nothing You ask for nothing but you always give your all

I cry because the years have not been kind I cry for I can not make it easier for you But I know with the love you have to share The love you give you receive back tenfold

Hi it's me again I'm home It's good to be home

It's great to see your smile It's great to see your face It's great to hear your voice It's great to feel your touch

But darlin' it only adds to your beauty

The beauty that only you have to give and share Ageing before your time has only made you look older But in looking older God has

Garry Gosney

given you a special gift
A special kinda beauty that only you can enhance

Controversial Dreams Wishes Hopes Lyrics

Good to Be Home

Hi it's me again I'm home It's good to be home

It's great to see your smile It's great to see your face It's great to hear your voice

It's great to feel your soft touch

It's great to be were my heart is at Were my heart has always called home It has finally brought us closer together Many miles apart have separated us

But our hearts have always been together

Hi it's me again I'm home It's good to be home

It's great to see your smile It's great to see your face It's great to hear your voice

It's great to feel your soft touch

I have finally met the country my heart loves A country that stole my heart and my love

So much to see and do and so much to catch up on But it's great to be home again

Will I stay or will I go a question I cannot answer

Hi it's me again I'm home It's good to be home

It's great to see your smile It's great to see your face It's great to hear your voice

It's great to feel your soft touch

But whichever way it goes I'm already at peace At peace for I have come home to my heart at last Now it's day by day just waiting for the right time The right time to be at ease with one's self and God The time is no longer an issue but the time is now For now I have completed a dream so now I am free

Hi it's me again I'm home It's good to be home

Garry Gosney

It's great to see your smile It's great to see your face It's great to hear your voice

It's great to feel your soft touch

Love you honey more than you will ever know

Controversial Dreams Wishes Hopes Lyrics

Tranquility of the Land

Looking at a strange place for the first time Seeing just what this strange land has to offer Or just what could I have to offer it

A country that is so vast and dangerous yet A country so peaceful and aw oh so beautiful

Just sitting watching a train move along Thinking just how beautiful this land really is I am a stranger to this wonderful land Strange yet oh so wonderful

Thinking just how many people ever really stop Stop to see what it is in the land to see

I could say not to many and I would be right

The peace and tranquility of the land The beauty in the mountains and towns To see a stream flowing though a town

The sounds of the birds and the call of nature

Just what is it that makes this strange land so So wonderful and oh so beautiful

The sounds of the creek at night The rustling of wind through the trees

The sounds of Mother Nature

God's creation and mother natures' beauty Just oh how the beauty shines just how

Just how could you ever improve on the sounds The sounds, the smells and sights of perfect beauty The beauty I have come to love in this strange Strange but exciting land

Garry Gosney

A Dream with a Meaning

Asked if I knew what I wanted out of life The answer is yes

I know what I want out of life I know what I like

And yes I will know it when I see them

It's hard to make someone understand the unknown For the unknown is not what they want to hear

But I guess the only way of putting it is Finding me going back to basics and rebuilding

Rebuilding a life and trying to find me Rebuilding the dream so I can put the pieces together

So many little dreams, but together they are only one dream One dream and one heart searching not for happiness...but...

One dream and one heart searching for peace and understanding

A stranger trying to see a new country for the first time Seeing the strange beauty it has to hold

Seeing life for the first time like a newborn baby Knowing and seeing hoping that a dream will come true

A dream that can end two ways one of happiness or one of sorrow

A dream is a wish your heart makes but it is only just a dream A dream with so much red tape governing the out come

A dream with a meaning and a purpose if only given a chance A chance to make a dream come true

But the most important thing is going back in time

In time to find out just who you are and what you have lost In time to find out just who you are and what you have to offer

Will this strange and wonderfully dangerous land give you a chance

A chance to open up your heart so that you find yourself A chance to make a dream come true

Controversial Dreams Wishes Hopes Lyrics

One dream and one heart searching for peace and understanding
Will it be found in this lifetime or is that just a dream too

Just what dream will come true

A dream of happiness or a dream of sorrow

Garry Gosney

Seem Like Heaven

Just the dark of night and stars an soft music Candle lit dinner for two by a babbling brook Just the two of us listening to the sounds

The sounds of the creek just flowing by The sound of water rushing over the rocks

The sound of the wind rustling through the trees

So many things that can make a night seem like heaven The stars shinning ever so bright against a full moon The sounds of the night owl calling for it's mate

Or the sounds of a platypus or beaver playing So many things to make it seem like heaven

So many things but I can only think of one

Only one thing that makes my world heaven and that is you For just being with you is heaven to me

I look into your eyes and I see the stars in the heavens I hold your hand and I feel the touch of an angel

So many things can make it seem like heaven

But heaven is holding you in my arms and kissing your lips Heaven is lying beside you and watching you sleep Heaven is being with the most precious of Gods creations God created heaven when he made you

But

So many things I want to say, but, The way you make me feel inside The pain and the hurt you give to me Just what is it that makes me still care

I went to see you but you did not show I rang but you did not answer

It's as though you don't even know I exist Just another person just one of many on your list

Many a time I think of you Just wanting to hate you but I can't

I can't for just knowing you is special The pain and joy you give to an old heart

Just so many things I want to say "but" But you do not hear for I am old

For you are young at heart and carefree Just what will it take to tame a heart

Tame a heart so young and beautiful Tame a heart so young and free

Free to roam in the beautiful heartlands Forever searching, forever free, but,

But you're always in my prayers and thoughts Something that not even you can destroy

For you are a special friend so young and free

Garry Gosney

A Dream No More

I want to look into your eyes and hold your hand Hold your hand and say nothing at all yet everything Walking hand in hand feeling your soft tender touch Looking into you eyes and seeing your sweet smile

A smile that said a thousand words Your eyes that paint a picture of beauty

I look and I see you only to find it's a dream

A dream but ever so special and beautiful never the less For maybe someday God willing you will be a dream no more

But a dream come true an answer to my prayers my angel

Wanting to kiss you and hold you tight Wanting to be with you

Wanting to see the picture in your eyes Wanting to read the words in your smile

Just maybe within time you will be a dream no more Just maybe within time you will be a dream come true Maybe someday you will be the answer to my prayers My angel sent down from the above

My imperfect beautiful angel, a dream come true A dream no more

A Scarred Heart

"I know you love him a long time ago" "Even now in my arms you still want him I know"

Even now in my heart I know you want him

Just what can I do to make you see

See just what your young heart means to me I am old but you show this old heart beauty A scarred heart so young and beautiful

A scarred heart so old heart and warn

Can the old and the young be united as one Can they see the beauty in each others scars A scarred heart young or old can it be healed Each has gone through a lot in there own way

Each life and each heart and each imperfection The beauty of the imperfect life

The beauty of the imperfect heart scarred but true The beauty of the imperfect imperfection

Just what can I do to make you see

See the hurt and the love you make me feel See the joy and sorrows that you give to me A old scarred heart caring for a beautiful

A beautiful young scarred imperfection An angel scared but a beautiful gift

A gift so beautiful God did not want to Want to improve on a beautiful scarred heart

Garry Gosney

Different Drums

Listening to the sounds of rain Listening to the sounds of the birds Listening to the sound of the wind Listening to the sounds of thunder

All I can think of is just

Just how beautiful nature really is Each sound has it's own beauty Each beat to a different drum

I watch the rainfall but it don't help

It can not wash away the pain you make feel I hear the thunder or is it my heart beating It is hard to tell for the pain is real

I see the birds singing their songs

I see the wind blowing through the trees But most of all I hear the beat of natures drum

Natures beat of different drums

The thunder only remind me of the beat of my heart The rain only remind me of the tears I cry

The birds only remind me of a voice of an angel The wind only reminds me of the love I give freely

A love given freely

Controversial Dreams Wishes Hopes Lyrics

Remember Where You Come From

Many things have changed some for the better Some for the worst but change never the less It can be for the better if it is handled right

It can be for the worst if done in the wrong hands But no matter which way it's done there is only Only one thing you must always remember "Remember where you come from"

For where you come from is who you are

It dose not matter were you go but where you come from It can be off the street with street smarts

It can be from the rich side of the educated world It can be from the right side of the tracks

But with out common sense and logic you have nothing Many people fall but not many can stand up again

We all need a hand from time to time

But you must remember where you have been

And how you got there but you may not like it but that's life It's Gods way of saying sorry for you have forgotten Forgotten where you came from and who you really are

Life is not easy for anyone rich or poor or the ones in the middle The rich have security checking on security so nothing is stolen

The one's in the middle class work hard but live out side their means The poor well the word speaks for it's self they have nothing of value But is it their fault or is it just the way God wanted it to be

Life's funny really in many ways the rich get rich of the poor The one's in the middle get rich of the poor too

But the ones that are the richest is the poor for their heart is always Always open forever lending a hand to those that need it most of all Never really questioning why for they know the mighty have fallen But it's their job to pick up the peaces you left behind

Garry Gosney

But the most important thing to remember is where you come from
For where you come from is you

For where you have been is you

For those that have helped you along your way is you

For you live with apart of every one you touch inside your heart
"Maybe it's God's way of saying thank you"

Thank you for all those that helped you along your way

Controversial Dreams Wishes Hopes Lyrics

Dream of a Thousand Tears

Looking out over the bay

Just listening to the sounds of the waves Seeing the seagulls flying and playing in the surf

Watching children playing in the sand Watching the smiles and laughter on their tiny faces

Thinking all the time about mine the ones I see no more I see them in my dreams

I hold them in my heart

I hear their voices through other children But it's just that holding on

Hanging on to something and can't let go just holding on

Should I hold on or should I let go

A thousand tears I cry for the answer I do not know A thousand tears I cry for the question I can't ask

A thousand tears I shed for the five faces I dream of Just what is in a dream of a thousand tears and heartache

Five beautiful children everyone special in their own way Each with faults but each hardened to the realities of life All before their time children turned into adults

Adults in children bodies just what have I done to them Each special and each my pride and joy and each a sorrow

I feel the wind and I see an eagle hovering by

I pray that strength of the eagle will guide you all I pray that the cunning of the wolf will be with you

But with each I give them my heart and love to share with you But most of all I pray God will find away to help you understand

Garry Gosney

Remember I Love You Always

Remember I love you always no matter where we are I just close my eyes and bring you near to me

Wish I could turn back the hands of time

In away that is true But in away it's not

For the conditions would be all changed Knowing what I know now would have changed some

But one thing I know will never change is my love

My love for you will never change for you are a part of me The circumstances are different now that I do know But not a day or night goes by with out loving you

The sounds of silence only broken by the sounds music Sounds of country music against the still of night Listening to songs trying to find a meaning to life But I shed a tear for you are the meaning to my life

For you gave me hope and give me the meaning to life Give for that's all you can do now from a far

For the circumstances are changed but my heart has not Maybe someday we can pick up the pieces of our torn hearts

I never promised you a rose garden in fact I promised nothing I promised nothing for that's is all I have to give

But I gave you my heart and love unconditionally and imperfect But most of all I gave you my heart freely imperfect as it is

I pray that one day we will find each other

I pray that one day our hearts will be united again as one I pray the God will find away to united us as one in family

Even if it's just holding you hand on passing the doors of life Remember I love you always and the door of my heart is always open

Controversial Dreams Wishes Hopes Lyrics

My World Changed

When your body touched mine it was special When your hand brushed against mine I was blessed

When I saw you and that look in your eyes When you touched your lips against mine

Just how your love makes my heart move My world changed

Oh how my world changed My world changed

Oh how my world changed

Just the thought of your body beside mine That soft oh soft touch of your skin on mine

Just how your body makes my heart move within Move like no other ever could or did

Just how your love makes my heart move My world changed

Oh how my world changed My world changed

Oh how my world changed

When I saw you and that look in your eyes A look that makes one feel special inside

That look of warmth and tenderness you have That look oh that look so rare a gift from God

Just how your love makes my heart move My world changed

Oh how my world changed My world changed

Oh how my world changed

Garry Gosney

The Fourth of July

I went to a Fourth of July bash at Crystal River Florida It was my first but I hope not my last

Just trying to see if I could get the feeling and meaning As an outsider it was not what one is lead to believe

What you hear on the local news and TV just didn't happen It was as though something was missing

It was as though they the people need reassurance in something I asked a young lady why she put an American flag on her car She said "to show patriotism"

I kinda cried inside and was hurt

Hurt to think that the 4th July is no more than just a name

Independence Day = a day of freedom Independence = freedom from control or influence of others

Liberty = (1) immunity from arbitrary exercise of authority,

Political independence

Freedom of choice

Personal freedom from servitude or confinement or oppression

Leave granted to a sailor of naval office

An act of undue intimacy

All I could think of was just how much freedom did America Did the American people really have or was it fake to Just how much and what do the people have a say in

Ever since I been here it has been about the government The government, the CIA, the fib, the newspapers, the TV

Everyone trying to score brownie points and out do each other But none giving the people the truth that they so seek answers to But they want you to die for them freely and ask no questions But they only tell

Controversial Dreams Wishes Hopes Lyrics

us / you half or part truths why are we not good

Not good enough for anyone in power to be honest with us

Do they have to hide behind red tape and not be made accountable?

Children get lost or stole but the departments and the governments People charged with petty crime get home detention and are aloud to work on it

People are put on home detention so long as they have a job and work A prisoner gets around 30.oo a week in side and no freedom as it's called jail

Jail for the corrupt and not home earning a full wage to support themselves Where is the justice you have stuff stolen or burnt but not get compen- sated for

But they are aloud to go home and do everyday things and earn a wage Again the government only tells you what they want us to know about independence

But at all times even the heads of government are not held responsible why After all it's there department employee that lost them and set the conditions

Is this the freedom we the people seek or the freedom they give us Just what price must we pay for our freedom and liberty before they? Before they give us the truth and the freedom our forefathers died for For that matter our children as well, as well as wives and husbands Just what is independence worth to each one of us

Just what is liberty worth to each of us

Just what price will the governments make us pay before the truth is told Just what is it we are afraid off

Or better yet what is it or are the governments afraid off Is it flying the flag to show patriotism

Or is it a country scarred and trying to hold on to something they never had Or holding on to a dream like I am or trying to make one come true But the true independence and liberty is the heart for no one can

Garry Gosney

take it Terrorist = characteristic of someone who employs terrorism (violence) (especially as a political weapon or tool)

Terrorist = hostile = (1) not belonging to your own counties forces or those of

an ally

Very unfavorable to life or growth

business) used to attempts to buy or take control of a business

marked by features that oppose constructive treatment or development

The love you give freely is your independence

The heart is your liberty and independence and nothing can destroy that

We are our own worst enemy but that does not mean we don't care for justice

For justice, for freedom, for liberty for all man kind,

For freedom to live and love as God intended as one with him not a flag

For in God we trust or do we

We do for he is our freedom, is our liberty, for he is the essence of all life

Lets remember the forth of July as the independence of the heart and a country

A country imperfect as it is but a country that each calls home for different reasons

A country imperfect as it is but a country that we call home

Controversial Dreams Wishes Hopes Lyrics

Garry Gosney

My First Fourth of July 2002

I went to a fourth of July bash in a small country town in Florida

It was my first but I hope not my last

Just trying to see if I could get the feeling and meaning As an outsider it was not what one is lead to believe

What you hear on the local news and TV just didn't happen It was as though something was missing

It was as though they the people need reassurance in something I asked a young lady why she put an American flag on her car She said "to show patriotism"

I kinda cried inside and was hurt

Hurt to think that the 4th July is no more than just a name

Independence Day = a day of freedom Independence = freedom from control or influence of others

Liberty = (1) immunity from arbitrary exercise of authority, political independence

freedom of choice

personal freedom from servitude or confinement or oppression

leave granted to a sailor of naval office

an act of undue intimacy

It is the first time in America and my first Fourth of July In fact my first in a lot of things in this wonderful land

Trying to see a country and trying to understand the beauty in it In many ways this is the saddest Fourth of July ever for many In many ways it was their first to

A first in that a love one was lost

A first in that it is the first after the world trade center disaster A first as in a country so proud was destroyed by terrorism or was it

Controversial Dreams Wishes Hopes Lyrics

A first that the world as we all knew it was destroyed Not only was the world destroyed as far as freedom went

It destroyed there heart as well my heart, my country, my home, my love It took away what I held so dear a love for my country

It took away what I held so dear a love to travel

It took away what I held so dear a love and a dream in a new country So many first like a newborn baby just what is going to happen

Will everything be alright just what is in store

So many questions and so many answers but still the first A Fourth of July with out love ones or family

A Fourth of July with out a country

A Fourth of July in a strange country searching for a meaning A meaning that for the first time had no meaning

For the first time for many a dream shattered

So many people and so many countries and so many firsts I cry I cry for the dead of the trade center and many that died trying

Trying to help clean up and selvage the impossible but trying never less Too many people worldwide will live with them in there hearts forever Forever as each shares a first we lost something in one way or another But we lost a peace of us a peace that we give to each other in time

In time of need we lend a hand we give a tear but still in god we trust It's a first for me but it's understandable as I feel lost in this country But lost and yet I feel secure, strange I know but the beauty I see I feel There is a beauty in knowing the first impressions do last

But the beauty is knowing God gave us the freedom we so deserve God gave it in the beauty of this countries landscapes

God gave it in the beauty of love God gave it in the beauty of the heart

We can all see the beauty in freedom if we close our eyes The beauty

Garry Gosney

of dreams, the beauty of the heart, the beauty of love The true independence and true liberty and true justice for all

A first for us but God gives it freely if only we see with our heart We will have the biggest Fourth of July ever

God bless the world for the world is the gift God gave us to enjoy Something no one can take away from us the gift

The freedom to belong, the freedom to roam, the freedom of the heart But most of all the freedom of love

My heart is still searching for the everlasting slice of freedom of life

Independence Day = a day of freedom = world freedom Independence = freedom from control or influence of others

Controversial Dreams Wishes Hopes Lyrics

Number One in Me

Friends once said my eyes are dead

Well in away I guess it's true in more ways than one They say the eyes are the windows to ones soul

They say the window to the world is though your eyes I wonder what it would be like to see the first time

I close my eyes and all I see is my children Each special and each number one in my heart

I close my eyes and see the only number ones in my life Only 5 that could ever be number one for they are me They are the best part of me the only part of me ever Friends say my eyes are dead well that could be so true Dead for I have nothing

Dead for I have lost the only ones that could ever matter Ever matter in my life or that will ever be number one to me The only ones that will ever matter or could ever matter

I no longer see as my world is dead

Now is just a dream a memory something to hold on to Just a name, a face, and a memory I will cherish forever Something that only I will see and the voices I hear

They will grow old as I will but the memory stays the same The same as the picture of their faces and the sounds

The sounds of their voices they will never die as we are one Number one in my heart

Number one in me something no one will ever change The number one in me

Garry Gosney

I Dream of

I dream dreams so sweet and true I dream of angels so sweet

I dream of perfect nights I dream of perfect days

I dream of the perfect imperfection I dream of you

I hear a voice say I am your angel Please don't cry for I am your angel

I can help you with your pain and sorrow I can help you for I am your angel

I dream dreams so sweet and true I dream of angels so sweet

I dream of perfect nights I dream of perfect days

I dream of the perfect imperfection I dream of you

I am imperfect but I was heaven sent Sent to show you that you are special Special in every sense of the word God's special angel imperfect as I am

I dream dreams so sweet and true I dream of angels so sweet

I dream of perfect nights I dream of perfect days

I dream of the perfect imperfection I dream of you

If a dream could come true

You're my dream come true a perfect imperfection I hear a voice say I am your angel

I am imperfect but I was heaven sent I dream dreams so sweet and true

I dream of angels so sweet I dream of perfect nights I dream of perfect days

I dream of the perfect imperfection I dream of you

Controversial Dreams Wishes Hopes Lyrics

A Gift With A F.L.A.W.

Every minute, every moment is a thought A thought of the most precious gift

A gift of friendship built on love A gift of love built on friendship A gift with a flaw

F = friend L = lover

A = awesome W = wonderful

A true gift that only a rose could enhance

Just what would it take to enhance you How can you be made better or more attractive

There is no way for the true you is inside The most attractive part is your scarred heart For ever scarred but for ever beautiful

No words can describe the way you make me feel No words can describe the beauty in you

No music can describe the way you make me feel No music can describe the beauty in you

For you are a gift

No photo can describe the way you make me feel No photo can describe the beauty in you

Just how can you capture a beautiful heart A heart so rare and oh so ever special

A true gift that only a rose could enhance

A gift with a flaw F = friend

L = lover A = awesome

W = wonderful

A true gift that only a rose could enhance Every minute, every moment I will love you From near and afar you will remain special

Garry Gosney

Oh so special and oh so rare and oh so beautiful For you are a true gift heaven sent Gods gift

For you are my friend

Controversial Dreams Wishes Hopes Lyrics

My Special Friends My Children

Not a day goes by that I don't think of you Thinking just what did I do to hurt you I'm living but it's a life with no meaning I'm living but it's a life with no purpose

Living inside a shell, living with a ghost me

I miss my friend more than life it's self My 5 special most beautiful children I know A ghost living in side of me drifting looking Looking for peace that for ever search of me For the day that I can be united with my kids

My best friend

Garry Gosney

Controversial Dreams Wishes Hopes Lyrics

A Ghost, a Shadow Without Meaning

"I'm just a ghost in this house" "I'm just a shell of a man I was"

"A living proof of a damaged heart breakup" "I'm just a whisper slow"

"I'm all that's left of two hearts on fire" "That once burned out of control" "Took my body and soul"

"I'm just a ghost in this house"

These WORDS are oh so True

Four walls made of bricks and wood just walls All the things that make up a house

But none that make a house a home just four walls Just wall with no meaning and no purpose Living and sharing with a ghost namely me

Sharing my life with a ghost Wandering where will it end or even a begin

Just what is in store I'm just a ghost living within Will I settle or will I drift through these walls Just what will it take to find peace in this house

Just how do you turn a house into a home

Just how do you turn four walls into a house to home Just how do you turn for wall into a meaning

How do you add purpose and meaning to a house to a home I'm just a ghost, a shadow without meaning or purpose

Garry Gosney

Controversial Dreams Wishes Hopes Lyrics

Sorrow but Happiness

Darlin' so much I want to say

Oh baby I know your dieing of cancer you told me so I see it in your eyes everyday

Darlin' it's out of my hands I know

I will never know what you are going though I only wish I could make you well

I pray that your wishes will come true Darlin' there was something about you that made

Made me fall for you

Darlin' each day I die a little with you

But baby girl I wouldn't have it any other way Just waking up to you makes life worthwhile Somehow we was brought together

But what ever the reason is or was I am great full For through you I have found happiness

Happiness in sorrow something I never knew possible But the more I see you

The more I thank God for each day with you I am blessed Blessed for each day your beauty grows more special Special for I care, special cause I've fallen for you

Falling for you more and more everyday I know it's hard to explain darlin'

But in loving you I found sorrow and happiness But I know in time I will loose you

Again sorrow but happiness for the treasured memories The treasured memories you gave me with your presents

Presents at my side

Garry Gosney

Promise

Darlin' I can promise you the world I can promise you the stars

But darlin' you already have them in your eyes I can promise you the moon

But it is in your smile

I can promise you the world

But darlin' you already have it at your fingertips I can promise you my love

I can promise you my heart

But darlin' you already have them with you But darlin'

Darlin' for the life in me I cannot give you

Give you one good reason to ever want the likes of me For I have nothing

But I have given all I have to give to you already Is it enough to keep you

OR

Is it enough to loose you

Darlin' only you can answer that question

Controversial Dreams Wishes Hopes Lyrics

Time Is Short

Why is it you always find someone who

Who captures your heart only when time is running out Why is it so is a test or is it something else

Just why are two hearts but together when time is short Is it meant to be or not just what is the reason in it

They say God gives and God takes away

Then why does he throw two hearts knowing time is short Just what can be achieved by it

Throwing into love only to be torn apart later on To be torn apart only by time and nothing more Time plays apart but will time be on their side

I hope so for time threw us together Now I hope time will keep us together Only time will tell

Garry Gosney

CHERISHED

One thing I have learnt over the years Cherish the moment

Cherish the one your with

Cherish the time you have for all it's worth For tomorrow it's just a memory

A cherished moment in time Cherish the silent moments together Cherish the quite walks together Cherish the cuddles

For they are all cherished moments in time Holding hands or looking in to their eyes A smile, a laugh just hearing them talk Seeing them cry all precious moments

A birth of a child or a death all precious Each to be cherished for what they are worth

Your precious moments in time cherished forever Forever for they are part of you

As you are part of me A true gift from god

A cherished memory "MINE"

God

God they say you care They say you know all They say you forgive all

They say you understand all They say you see all

They say most of all you love all

God I would like you to do me a favor Take my life and give it to the one who Who stole my heart

Take my arms and wrap her up in them for comfort Take my heart and place it beside hers for company Take my hand and place her hand in mine to show I'm there for her

Take my love and give it to her for all time

God I don't believe in miracles

For the miracle I need is far too great for anyone I'm not perfect so I will only ask for a favor They say you hear all prayers

They say you answer all

If it is true it will take the biggest miracle miracle of all time

So many little things to make one picture God

Will that imperfect picture of love ever Ever be taken

Garry Gosney

Shooting Star

I see a shooting star ever so beautiful Ever so graceful as it lights up the night sky They say you see a falling star to make a wish

They say catch a falling star, your dream comes true

Well darlin' I saw a shooting star and wished Wished I could make you believe I love you

Wished that I could make you understand how much I care Wished that someday you will see with your heart

Well darlin' I captured a falling star and dreamt

Well that's not true for you captured me with your baggage an all I know time is hard and life will not be a bed of roses

But a rose has thorns each thorn a step up to a beautiful rosebud

But darlin' I see a rose I see you Two of Gods beautiful creations

I see the stars and I see three beautiful creations I see a shooting star and all I can do is wish

I can make you as happy as you make me

Lady girl I Love You my way Your baggage is part of you

Your wonderful children are part of you Lady Girl

Whatever you have is all right with me In time we can work it all out

For you are my shinning star my dream come true An imperfect dream it may be

For just being with you is my slice of heaven

Controversial Dreams Wishes Hopes Lyrics

My Everything My All

"Where would you be" "If you were not with me" "Where would you go"

Where would I be without you the ANSWER to that is LOST

If I was not with you

I would leave you my heart For I would have no use for it

Where would I go

That is the million dollar question For wherever I go you there with me

You tears, your smile, your looks Your voice, all go where I go

Every town, every corner I turn I see you I cry myself to sleep thinking of you

I wake up crying just thinking of you Even the rain can not wash away Wash away the tears I cry inside

I cry, I pray, I cry but no one understands Understands just what you mean to me With you "you" make me feel alive

Without you I am just a ghost an empty shell For you are my everything my all

Garry Gosney

ONE

One just a number without ????? one = ????

one = bird one = tree one = cow one = heart one = human

Just a number without meaning or purpose

Two = one plus one two = birds two = trees

two = cows two = hearts two = humans

Just a number with a meaning

Three = two plus one = meaning plus purpose Four or more all adds to the meaning and purpose For after all one is not one anymore

One is a family in love and in heart Friends are fine that is true

But

Family make ONE the happiest number alive

My Mountain Home

There is a peace in the mountains Like no other it's rugged yet smooth

The trees add to the smoothness of them The winds blow at a howling pace

But it just adds to the beauty of the mountains Watching the trees and listening to the thunder Seeing the trees change colour is great

But seeing a whole mountain top change is awesome The peace of the mountain broken only by the roar thunder The peace of the mountains broken by the howl of the wind The tranquility broken by the laughter of children and families

But all in all they make the mountains

The tranquility broken only by the sounds of nature Is it a special kind of person that lives there

Is it a necessity or is it out of love for nature Some say both and I would agree with them But I think love has more to do with it

It's a freedom it's away of life like no other Waking up to the sounds and sites of nature at it's best

Forever changing mountains

A mountain forever dangerous yet respectful A mountain a home to so many

A luxury to so few But

A heaven to me my mountain home

Garry Gosney

OWN

One can never own anyone

We can love them for what they are To own someone is to imprison them Imprison them into something there not

For no matter what you do you will never own them You can own a body but you will never own the heart For the heart is given freely for you care

For you love them so your heart is given freely For you stay because you want to

Not because you have to

Your heart is free so will always roam But it's like your love it's given freely

If you are true to your heart you will stay For you stay because you are free Married but free

Single but free A couple but free

Free to roam, free to love, but still find it's way Way home to the one you gave your heart to every day

Darlin' I stay because I want to

I stay because I am free to love you I stay because I care

I stay because I want to out of love for you Darlin' I love you for just being you

Nightmare of Tears

Many times I shed a tear

Mostly because I can't be where I want to be Mostly because I can't be with the ones I love I miss the lady who stole my heart

I miss my children and parents But most of all I miss my lady The days are all ok

It's like everyone is at work or at school Then the night falls and the tears start All I do is picture their faces and smiles

But it's all to no avail the tears just flow more just when will they stop

How many tears must you shed

To get rid of the empty hollow feeling inside Or

Is it just a nightmare of tears that will never stop

Garry Gosney

The Saddest Song of All

I listen to the sounds of music

Some modern, some classic but mostly country Oh how they sing

Rogers: Strait: Tennison: Martina: Allan: Loanstar: the list is endless Oh how they sing with the grace and beauty of the angels

Oh how they sing they take a plain song and make it beautiful They write and sing with the grace and beauty of the angels But the saddest song of all is the one I can't write for you

For I love you so oh how I love you so

I can't find the words to write the song that you make my heart sing I say the words over and over but I just can't find the words

I say them but I just can't add the grace and beauty to them

I say them but I don't sing them with the grace and beauty you deserve

Oh how they sing they take a plain song and make it beautiful They write and sing with the grace and beauty of the angels But the saddest song of all is the one I can't write for you

For I love you so oh how I love you so

The way you make my heart sing at the sight of your name The way you make my heart sing at the sound of your voice The way you make my heart dance when it sees you

Oh how I would love to write you a song

Oh how they sing they take a plain song and make it beautiful They write and sing with the grace and beauty of the angels But the saddest song of all is the one I can't write for you

For I love you so oh how I love you so

A song of beauty and grace fit for an angel Oh how you make my heart sing

Controversial Dreams Wishes Hopes Lyrics

Oh how you make my heart dance Oh darlin' I love you so

Oh how I would Love to rite the perfect song for you

Rogers: Strait: Tennison: Martina: Allan: Loanstar: the list is endless

Oh how they sing they take a plain song and make it beautiful They write and sing with the grace and beauty of the angels But the saddest song of all is the one I can't write for you

For I love you so oh how I love you so

But the saddest song of all is the one I can't write for you For I love you so, oh how I love you so

Garry Gosney

My Heart No More

Lonely days and lonely nights Oh just how much I miss you Lonely hours and lonely minutes I just wish you could understand

Understand just how much you mean to me Each minute without you is time lost Each hour without you my heart aches Each day with out you my heart cries Each night without you is a nightmare

But I see you standing there out of reach Darlin' no matter what you have a piece of my heart Darlin' I give you my heart to hold and look after Lonely days and lonely nights I know my heart is safe

For it is with the one I love My heart no more

Controversial Dreams Wishes Hopes Lyrics

Every Time

Every time I want to love you You come up with a reason to stop me

I know I Am Poor

I know I have nothing to offer you

I know I can never give you what you deserve

But it has never stopped me from loving you I can only love you my way

I can only give you me Not much I know

No job, no security, no nothing but darlin' Darlin' I can only give you me and my love

Every time I want to love you You come up with a reason to stop me

I know I Am Poor

I know I have nothing to offer you

I know I can never give you what you deserve

Many a tear I shed but it's pointless Pointless for the butterflies you seek are missing

Is it because we are older or what Just what are the butterflies we seek

Or is it our values and outlook on life that has changed

Every time I want to love you You come up with a reason to stop me

I know I Am Poor

I know I have nothing to offer you

I know I can never give you what you deserve

Just what are the butterflies of love Just what are the butterflies of comfort Just what are the butterflies of belonging

Just what are the butterflies of understanding Just what are the

Garry Gosney

butterflies of happiness

Just what are the butterflies we seek

Every time I want to love you You come up with a reason to stop me

I know I Am Poor

I know I have nothing to offer you

I know I can never give you what you deserve

Controversial Dreams Wishes Hopes Lyrics

Sparkle

The thought of waking up to you Is a dream come true

Waking up to see the sunrise every morning Is a dream come true

Seeing the sunset every night Is a dream come true

For you are my sunrise and a delight For you are my sunset and a delight

I see you in the sunrise and it enhances your beauty I see you in the sunset and it enhances your beauty I see the sun and feel the warmth it gives to you

I see the moon and I see just how beautiful God made you I see the stars and I see your eyes oh how they sparkle But darlin' you don't need the stars to sparkle

For you sparkle every time I see you But then I am biased for

I Love You

Garry Gosney

The Ghost That Prayers

Just how does one compete with a love that's not wanted Just how can you compete for a love that's one sided

Just what are you up against Just what is it that is missing

Every time I turn around I see your face and smile Every voice I hear is your voice

Just how can I compete when your fighting every more I make I'm in love with you a ghost in my imagination

The imagination darlin' is real for the ghost is real

You have my heart but God has my soul but you are my all Your my heart and soul and my reason for living your my all No-matter what I do I can not forget you for you are my all

Many miles and oceans may separate us but my heart is with you With you in the heartland of love watching every move you make Watching just to make sure your safe for I care

Care cause I miss you so much more that you will ever know

You may not want it but darlin' I can not deny what's in my heart I can not stop the way my feels or deny the love I have for you

You're the ghost in my heart but darlin'

I'm the ghost that watches over you to keep you safe

I'm the ghost that prayers for your safety and guidance and understanding I'm the ghost that prayers that someday you will find the happiness you seek

The happiness that you brought to this old fool in love with you

But in the mean time I'm the ghost that prayers and watches over you I love you darlin'

FROM

The ghost that prayers

Controversial Dreams Wishes Hopes Lyrics

She Is

There is a lady in the mountains Who makes the mountains her home

But she is just as pretty if not more beautiful But then she is beautiful no-matter where she is

She is shy, she is woman, she is pretty, and she is She is mischievous, everything that makes her special Her smile, her eyes the list is long and oh so beautiful

But they are the thing's that made me fall for her

Only a rose could enhance her beauty Only a carnation could soften her beauty But no-matter what she dose

She has brought joy to my life

She has a piece of my heart to hold A piece to comfort her wherever she is Darlin' where ever you go for all time

For all time lady gal for you are my best friend

She Is

Garry Gosney

Existence

I let my heart travel when I was young I stayed and lived an existence

A stranger in my homeland with no heart

I went to school with no heart I worked with no heart

I married with no heart

But I have 5 beautiful children that have my love They have my love but not all my heart

I finally landed in the country that has my heart

I met someone who has my heart but they threw it away So I have my heart no more

It's normal for me as it's all I have ever known

A stranger existing without a heart

A stranger in a strange land that has my heart Just who am I kidding for I already know the truth

I know I'm destined to a life without a heart An existence, a stranger without a heart

Controversial Dreams Wishes Hopes Lyrics

11 September 2002 A Year Ago Today

I miss the look of surrender in your eyes

But most of all I miss my friend

I miss the tough of your hand in mine I miss the smile you gave me every day

But most of all I miss the most important thing of all "YOU" I miss the love you gave to me and the love we shared

A year ago today I kissed you on the cheek A year ago today I held your hand in mine

A year ago I said darlin' I love you and see you tonight A year ago I said I loved you that was a year ago

Well the year has past and the tears are still flowing

The year has past and not a day goes by that a tear is not shed I shed a tear for you cause I miss my heart, and my friend

I shed a thousand more for I cannot be with you

Darlin' you have my heart and the children say hi to you every night They say life must go one that is true I know for I know you want me to To march on and make our home even better for I know your our angel Our guardian angel the love of my life like no other

God giveth and God taketh but darlin' even though you're gone you still live For through our children and my heart your memories will live forever This home is your home you own it I am just a keeper

I light a candle in our home I light a candle in our hearts for ever

God do me a favour and give our love ones the love and eternal life Eternal life and the gift of the angels that they so deserve

I can not prayer enough or stop the tears I shed for love ones lost For love ones lost a year go today darlin' I miss you and love you so

God bless everyone and the world one year later God bless take care A

Garry Gosney

year ago today you had my heart

A year ago today you touched the hearts of the world A lifetime from now you will be in my heart

Controversial Dreams Wishes Hopes Lyrics

This Land My Home

From Vancouver Canada to Oregon and everything in between From Oregon To West Virginia to Florida and in between

The land is vast and rugged but yet oh so beautiful It's a strange land in many ways but oh so beautiful The mountains, the plains, the hills

Each add their own kind of beauty to this country my home Each breed their own kind of people

A breed like no other but each special in there own right A place with a sunset a glow

Each town different but oh so unique Each breed their own people

Each proud to be part of something unique Unique yet oh so special and oh so beautiful

The changing of the leaves and the changing of the seasons Each mountain, each hill, each plain each beautiful to see Each part of a beautiful country

Florida to Oklahoma to Iowa have something to be proud of Each have something to be enjoyed

Something to call home

The beauty of this land my home

Garry Gosney
Happy Birthday

Sitting here listening to my favourite songs Thinking of what can I give a beautiful woman But there is a catch I am poor and

She is so beautiful She is so special to me

She is my friend, my sister, and much much more

All I can think of is my love for you and what you do to me Thinking off what you really mean to me

It was no accident me finding you Someone had a hand in it, long before ever knew

Now I just can't believe your in my life Heavens smiling down me, as I look at you tonight

I tip my hat, to the keeper of stars

He sure knew what he was doing when he joined these two hearts I hold everything, when I hold you in my arms and I've got all I'll ever need thanks to the Keeper of the Stars

Soft moonlight on your face, oh how you shine

It takes my breath away, just to look into your eyes

All I can think of is how beautiful you are in your own way All I can think off how you make me feel inside

Here is a copy of sticker I brought it kinda said it all

B = Beautiful I = Intelligent T = Talented C = Charming

H = Horny

This in many many ways made me love you just the way you are

One word that's all you said Something in your voice caused me To turned my head, your smile

Just captured you and me were in my future

Far as I could see and I don't know how it happened But it happens

Controversial Dreams Wishes Hopes Lyrics

still, You ask me if I love you

If I always will... Well... You had me from "Hello"

I felt love start to grow, the moment that I looked into your eyes You won me, it was over from the start

You completely stole my heart and now you won't let go

I never even had a chance you know you had me from "Hello"

All I could think off is what could I possibly have to give you All I have is me and that's all

All I have is nothing but my love for you All I can think off is dose she feel the same All I can think off will she like what I have Thousands off miles apart but my love is real

Our love is unconditional we knew it from the start I see it in your eyes you can feel it in my heart

From here on after lets stay the way we are right now And share all love and laughter that a lifetime will allow I cross my heart and promise to

Give all I've got to give to make all your dreams come true In all the world you'll never find a love as true as mine

Happy Birthday to you beautiful lady Happy Birthday and may all your dreams come true

Happy Birthday darlin' this is your day to be

The biggest BITCH you can (wink wink) but your beautiful anyways This is your time to be happy your special day of days

It only comes once a year

I am sad I can not be there on this special day or any other But you have my love with you and always will

Take care, take care beautiful lady You deserve more than I can give HAPPY BIRTHDAY

Ti Amo

Garry Gosney

Controversial Dreams Wishes Hopes Lyrics

Oh What a Lady

There is a lady she is smart There is a lady she is plain

There is a lady average in everyway Her height is perfect just as she is There is a lady oh what a lady

She is an educated lady very smart She is just as smart as her beauty

But the best part of her is what she don't like (her fat) as she puts it but when you see her You see just how beautiful she is

She is tall, but oh what a lady, what a lady What a lady so pure in heart and oh so loveable To hold her in your arms is a pure delight

Oh what a lady to cuddle that (her fat) is joy To let her go is pure agony hell on earth

Oh what a lady just watching her smile and laugh Thinking over just how we meet what made us do Made us do what we did and what brought us together Was it fait or was it a cruel joke on someone's part

But whatever the reason I'm happy to have held her in my arms

I got to hold and love an educated woman oh what a woman Just what was I thinking a distinguished lady a real woman Just what was I thinking I who have nothing to offer her

I can not do her beauty justice for she is educated and I am not How can I compete for the hand and the heart of an educated lady

I who have nothing to offer her beauty but my love

I who have nothing to offer the distinguished lady but my heart

I who have nothing to offer her but me and I'm imperfect in every way I am dyslexic and she is educated so why would she want the likes of me

The world is your oyster darlin' go get you pearl

Hold your head up high darlin' be afraid of no man for you are beautiful You are beautiful in body and heart darlin' go get your

Garry Gosney

slice of heaven Just remember I love you and am proud and honored to hold you in my arms

Darlin' you are one special woman oh what a lady you are (my slice of heaven)

Darlin' I have no rite to hold you back go get you pearl

I will shed a tear or two for sure but they will be for both joy and sorrow Tears of joy for I got to see your beauty in every way

Tears of sorrow for you are one distinguished woman oh what a lady you are

I am no-one of importance you are a lady a distinguished and educated woman

Please remember teacher, distinguished lady, I Love You...Oh What A Lady

Oh What a lady...love you darlin' Oh what a WOMAN you are

Controversial Dreams Wishes Hopes Lyrics

Just How Can I

She asked me if I was fine if everything was alright She asked as to show she cares or is interested

But how do you tell someone you love How do you tell the one who has your heart

How do you tell them that you're crying within Crying for you cannot be with the one you love them

The one you have given your heart freely too The one you hold every moment in your heart

The one you close your eyes and kiss goodnight too every night The one you close your eyes and kiss good morning too everyday The one that is with you every were you go even in your dreams

Just how do you tell her you cried yourself to sleep at night Just how do you tell her you cried yourself awake everyday Just how can I tell her the thousand tears I shed are for her Just how can I

What is it that I need to do, just what is it I'm doing wrong

I say a prayer but God dos not hear me the tears will not stop I pray but what for the tears I cry inside just flow deeper and faster I pray that my heart will be with her to comfort her

I pray that my heart will give her the strength and the love she needs

Just how can I...I can not...so I tell a lie...that I'm fine with a smile But I will give her my heart and my love everyday and wait for her return

I will pray that she is always kept safe and that God

God will give her my heart strengthens her weakness and comforts her strengths

Maybe then she will rest in the comfort of my arms and my love and accept my heart

Just how can I...tell her I'm crying a thousand tears for I love her Just how can I...I can not...so I tell a lie...that I'm fine with a smile Just how

Garry Gosney

can I...I can not...

Controversial Dreams Wishes Hopes Lyrics

Garry Gosney

Controversial Dreams Wishes Hopes Lyrics